Christianity in the Roman World

Christianity
in the Roman World

R. A. MARKUS

with 74 illustrations and a map

CHARLES SCRIBNER'S SONS

NEW YORK

PHOTOGRAPHIC ACKNOWLEDGEMENTS

Author: 16, 17, 34, 35, 36, 38, 40, 48, 49, 53, 57, 68, 71, 74; *Osualdo Böhm:* 18; *Fototeca Unione:* 1, 73; *Deutsches Archäologisches Institut, Rome:* 8, 10, 13, 56; *Friedrich Hewicker:* 25; *Hirmer Verlag:* 11, 21, 23, 27, 32, 58, 65, 67, 69, 70; *Islay de Lyons:* 6; *Mansell Collection:* 4, 5, 9, 12, 14, 15, 28, 29, 30, 31, 33, 39, 41, 42, 43, 44, 59, 61; *Pont. Comm. di Arch. Sacra:* 24; *Gisela Richter:* 66; *Rheinisches Museum, Trier:* 37; *Guido Sansoni:* 2; *Staatsbibliothek, Bamberg:* 64; *Zumbühl:* 52.

1 3 5 7 9 11 13 15 17 19 I/C 20 18 16 14 12 10 8 6 4 2

Printed in Great Britain
Library of Congress Catalog card Number 74-16823

ISBN 0-684-14129-9

Contents

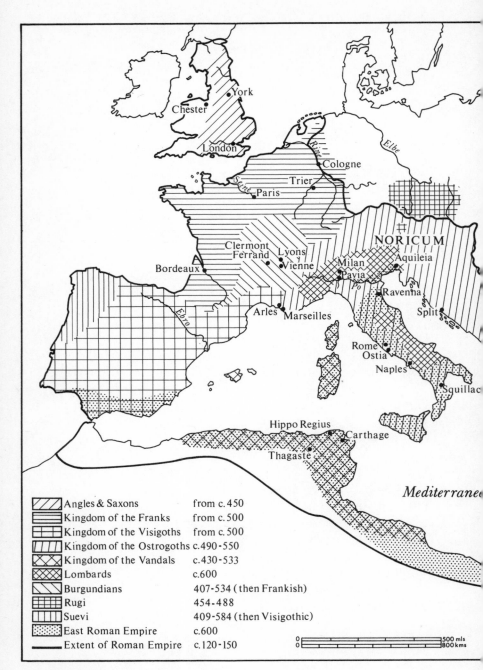

York
Chester
London
Cologne
Trier
Paris
Seine
Rhine
Elbe

NORICUM

Clermont
Ferrand
Lyons
Vienne
Bordeaux
Milan
Pavia
Po
Aquileia
Ravenna
Split

Arles
Marseilles
Ebro

Rome
Ostia
Naples
Squillac

Hippo Regius
Carthage
Thagaste

Mediterranee

Angles & Saxons	from c. 450
Kingdom of the Franks	from c. 500
Kingdom of the Visigoths	from c. 500
Kingdom of the Ostrogoths	c. 490-550
Kingdom of the Vandals	c. 430-533
Lombards	c. 600
Burgundians	407-534 (then Frankish)
Rugi	454-488
Suevi	409-584 (then Visigothic)
East Roman Empire	c. 600
Extent of Roman Empire	c. 120-150

0 500 mls
0 800 kms

The Roman World to *c.* AD 600.

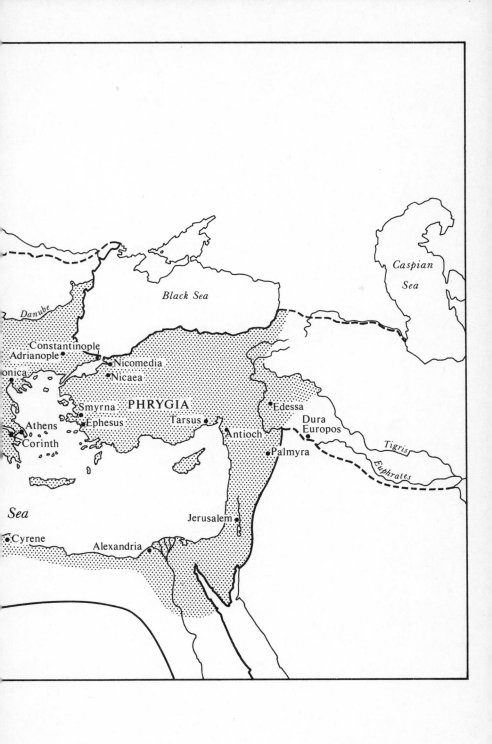

Preface

'IN THE DAYS OF HEROD, the king of Judaea' (Luke 1:1); 'in the fifteenth year of the reign of Tiberius Caesar, Pontius Pilate being governor of Judaea' (Luke 3:1): with such phrases the Gospel insistently reminds the Christian believer of the geographical and historical setting of the beginnings of Christianity. There is more than one way of telling the history of Christian origins, of the early development of Christianity, of its spread around the Mediterranean world during the first centuries of our era and the history of the internal development of the Christian group. Whichever way we approach it, the Roman world is part of the story. From the point of view of the historian of the ancient world Christianity will be a very minor strand at first, a footnote to the more dramatic history of a perpetually troubled region, Palestine. It will claim more of his attention as the movement grows. By the time he comes to deal with the fourth century he will not be able to bypass its importance in public affairs. But throughout, one strand among many themes its history will remain. For the traditional Church historian the same story will, of course, be of focal interest; and the focus will be narrower still for the historian of Christian belief or worship, of Christian literature or art. For all these, whatever their specialized interests, the Roman world must provide the permanent context. For the first five or six hundred years it was the matrix of Christianity. At the very beginning, the 'Roman world' stands for a small corner of the Empire of Augustus; for Judaea and Galilee, a Roman province administered by a Roman procurator and an area ruled by a

8

native prince with allegiance to the Empire. Before long, Syria, Asia Minor and regions further afield come into the picture. At some time between 300 and 600 the whole Empire has become the setting of Christianity. It is true that during that period Christianity was carried beyond the imperial frontiers and managed to take root here and there outside the Roman Empire, both on its Eastern and Western fringes. For all that, we need not minimize the importance of such Christian outposts to appreciate that until, roughly, the end of the sixth century the history of Christianity is in the main its history in the Roman world.

The period covered in this book is that during which Christianity may be considered as substantially coextensive with the Roman world. I have not, however, tried to write either a history of the Christian Church in this period or of the Roman world as its setting. Excellent accounts of both are available. The interested reader will find some of them among my bibliographical suggestions. Still less have I confined my attention to the narrower subject of the relations between the Roman State and the Christian Church. My purpose has been to describe Christian life and thought, and their varied expressions in terms of their interplay with the non-Christian world. To put it another way, I have tried to trace the history of Christian self-awareness in the Roman world, the ways in which Christians saw themselves as a distinct group in society, the ways in which they identified themselves with it – its structures, its values, its culture – and the ways in which they opposed themselves to or differentiated themselves from it.

Thus, about two-thirds of the way through our period, in the year 417, a Christian native of Roman Spain, who had left home to travel to Roman Africa (and was to go on further east) wrote: 'When I, a refugee from disturbance and upheaval, flee to a haven of security, I find everywhere my native land, everywhere my law and my religion. . . . As a Christian and as a Roman, it is to Romans and to Christians I come.'[1] Orosius' effortless conflation of his Roman with his

Preface

Christian identity marks one phase in the history of Christian self-awareness in the Roman world. It had not always been a possible one, and not everywhere; nor did all Christians choose this option. From the earliest times of the Christian community, its members were aware of having a special identity in their world; but the forms of that awareness underwent profound changes.

One besetting temptation, to which both secular and ecclesiastical historians are exposed, is to assume that in the relationship between Christianity and the secular world around it 'Christianity' stands for a fixed quantity. Church historians, especially, looking back at the early phases of a development, the eventual outcome of which they cannot help knowing, are apt to take the identity of the Christian group too much for granted. Though they are, of course, ready enough to see it as always changing, always developing, they also assume too easily that what is changing and developing is something given and easily discernible. 'Christianity' tends to become the name for an underlying substance, a 'supposed I-know-not-what' which supports the historically changing accidents and relationships with what lies outside it. It will be part of my intention to exhibit the growing self-awareness of Christians as crystallized in their confrontation with what they came to recognize as non-Christian only in the moments of dawning self-definition. An overwhelming loyalty to the Lord who had died and risen again, an irresistible call to confess him before the world, gave the earliest Christians a clear sense of what distinguished them from their fellow-men. All who called themselves 'Christians' shared a general sense of being followers of Jesus Christ; but this soon proved insufficient to define their identity to their own satisfaction. From almost the first moments of its perceptible existence the Christian group was tension-ridden; some of its members appeared in the eyes of others as Christians in name only, as counterfeits of the reality. The conflict with the 'false brother' is the obverse of the process of self-discovery. Thus in Chapter 3 we shall consider the crisis in which 'orthodox' Christianity differentiated itself from wider circles which also professed some sort of belief in Jesus Christ. In this situation Christians became aware of a profound threat to what they considered to be the essential kernel of their Christianity from groups who also professed themselves – in varying ways and to varying degrees – to be followers of Jesus Christ. The confrontation between these 'gnostic' groups and Christian 'orthodoxy' was as much a phase in crystallizing Christian self-awareness as a conflict between 'Christian' and what came to be recognized as non-Christian only in the confrontation.

In the varying relationship between Christianity and the secular world around it both partners are always undergoing change. The primary awareness men have of their world is always shaped as much by the forms of their own traditions of perception as by the forms of the world they encounter; both were changing profoundly in the centuries I shall be concerned with. I shall try to sketch some of the more momentous of these changes, riding roughshod over a great many nuances and variations, following my own sense of what is important. That great historian, Norman Baynes, once remarked on the difficulty of mapping the primary shifts in men's consciousness: 'One is tempted to say that the more significant a movement is the less adequately can we as students of history explain it.' Baynes's warning should not deter us from trying to understand the profound transformations in the modes of Christian self-understanding during the early centuries; but it should serve as a reminder of the dangers that attend the task. I know I have not escaped them all. I offer my interpretation with a due sense that wilfulness and distortion are ever-present perils and that it behoves the historian to remain tentative.

To Christopher Brooke, at whose instigation this book was written, the book owes much more than its existence, and I very much more than an author can ever have owed to the general editor of a series. I wish also to record here my gratitude to Gervase Mathew, the first of my teachers to reveal to me the fascination of the late Roman and early Christian world; to Hilary Armstrong, whose friendship and deep knowledge of this period have given me much nourishment over the years, and whose suggestions have helped me to avoid many pitfalls; to Sabine MacCormack, who has placed her extensive knowledge of late Roman art and ideology unstintingly at my disposal; to several generations of my pupils in the Liverpool University School of History, to whom the book owes more than any of them can realize; to the superintendents of antiquities and museums too numerous to list here, who have been generous with time and effort on my behalf, and to Anna Fazzari of the British School at Rome who straightened my way to many of their doors; to Frank and Anne Kennedy, who have helped to make a small part of my work the greatest pleasure; and to my wife and my colleagues, who, as always, have borne the burden and the heat of the day.

Liverpool   R.A.M.

CHAPTER ONE

A sect among sects

WHEN the Roman historian Tacitus wanted to identify
Christianity for his readers, he described it as the group
which followed a leader who had been executed under the
governor of Judaea, Pontius Pilatus, during the reign of
Emperor Tiberius.[1] Tacitus was writing early in the second
century. During the first half of that century the Roman
Empire attained the height of its power and prosperity.
Stretching from northern Britain to the Euphrates, from the
Rhine and the Danube to the Atlas Mountains, it reached its
greatest extent. Conquests fed a buoyant economy; a stable
and self-confident society created a cosmopolitan culture.
We have a speech by a Greek orator celebrating its achieve-
ments on the occasion of a visit to Rome around the year 150.
Addressing his audience in a Greek which he could assume
to be familiar to them he said:

. . . the present empire has been extended to boundaries of no mean
distance. . . . Now all the Greek cities rise up under your leadership,
and the monuments which are dedicated in them and all their
embellishments and comforts redound to your honour like beautiful suburbs. The coasts and interiors have been filled with cities,
some newly founded, others increased under and by you.

Taking good care of the Hellenes as of your foster parents, you
constantly hold your hand over them, and when they are prostrate,
you raise them up. . . . The barbarians you educate. . . .

As on holiday, the whole civilized world lays down the arms
which were its ancient burden and has turned to adornment and
all glad thoughts, with power to realize them. All other rivalries
have left the [cities], and this one contention holds them all, how
each city may appear most beautiful and attractive. All localities

are full of gymnasia, fountains, monumental approaches, temples, workshops, schools, and one can say that the civilized world, which had been sick from the beginning, as it were, has been brought by right knowledge to a state of health.[2]

The zenith of the achievement here celebrated by Aelius Aristides had been reached during his own lifetime. The Romans had long ago come into control over Italy; after a series of desperate wars with Carthage, the leading power in the Western Mediterranean, and after the conquest of the remnants of the great empire built up by Alexander the Great, North Africa, Spain, Greece, Asia Minor, the Middle East and Egypt had all come under Roman control. The conquests of Alexander had brought the Eastern Mediterranean and its borderlands within the orbit of the Greek language, and within reach of the most characteristic products of Greek civilization: the Greek city and its culture, and a way of life in which urban institutions played an important part. Rome had stepped into the legacy of Alexander's empire. With the extension of her sway in Western Europe, the Roman Empire became the medium through which the main achievement of Hellenistic civilization was diffused over Europe. Educated Westerners were as conscious as Aelius Aristides that Rome was the beneficiary of the Hellenistic heritage. Latin joined Greek as the *lingua franca* of Europe, Africa, and Asia bordering the Mediterranean; urban institutions followed in the wake of conquering Roman armies and planted the seeds of a Mediterranean civilization among a great variety of local cultures.

The Roman Empire was the co-existence of many peoples with their diverse cultures under the sway of the 'Roman peace'. From the viewpoint of an educated, aristocratic Roman some of these must have looked very outlandish. Tacitus had little liking for the Jews, a turbulent people in a remote Eastern province, with their peculiar and exclusive religious ideas and practices. Yet their existence was taken for granted and Romans had long been used to Judaism among the many odd customs, ideas and religions current within the Empire. By its very imperialism, Rome was committed to a tolerant hospitality towards national and local cults. Even the Jewish religion, so long as it did not feed the flames of revolt, was acceptable, despite its exclusiveness and – in many Roman eyes – unseemliness. The Jews and Judaism were familiar to Romans as part of their inheritance through conquest of the Eastern Mediterranean world. But Christianity was another matter.

Its founder had been a Jew, born under the Emperor Augustus and executed some thirty years later under Tiberius. The sect, to the horror of Tacitus, revived, despite the execution of its leader, and its adherents had reached Rome, the capital where 'all degraded and shameful practices flow together'. What made this new sect difficult for a Roman to understand, when it appeared on the Roman scene, was its peculiar relationship to Judaism. It belonged to the Jewish milieu while trying, at the same time, to disown its ancestry, and being disowned by most of the race of its progenitors. Tacitus, like many others, found this puzzling; but puzzlement apart, his story – though told from an outsider's point of view – is identical with the story told by the third Evangelist. Luke's narrative begins 'in the days of Herod, the King of Judaea' and ends, in the second instalment of his account, with St Paul preaching in Rome. By that time the Gospel Paul was preaching had been heard in several major cities in the Greek-speaking part of the Roman world. We should not under-estimate the difficulty an educated pagan would have experienced around the turn of the first century in distinguishing the Christians from other groups originating among the Jews; and the perspective of nineteen centuries should not blind us to the extent to which Christians themselves would have shared the pagan's uncertainties. In this first chapter we shall look – very briefly – at the way in which Christianity became aware of itself in its first historical milieu, within Judaism.

At the time of Augustus, Judaism was no simple monolithic entity. Looked at geographically, its core lay in

Palestine, the Jews' ancient homeland; but most of the Hellenistic cities had their colonies of Jewish settlers. Often they were well-established groups and in some places, for instance in Alexandria, they formed a large minority in the local population. This melting-pot of Greek and Near-Eastern cultures had become a leading centre of Hellenized Judaism. Jews of the 'Dispersion' (Diaspora), though careful to maintain their religious identity, assimilated much of the culture of the society around them. In Alexandria their Bible had long been read in a Greek translation. An outstanding Jewish scholar such as Philo, more or less contemporary with Christ, could be well abreast of his gentile contemporaries in his knowledge of the literature and thought of the Greek world. His approach to the exposition of the Old Testament differed little from the current fashions of expounding the stories of Homer and the Olympian mythology. The 'spiritual' truths he discovered hidden in the scriptures with the aid of allegorical interpretation were part of the common stock of philosophical ideas circulating in the Hellenistic world.

Philo was not only a Hellenistic scholar but also a strictly observant Jew. In his own person he illustrates the strength of a religious loyalty which kept alive the Jew's sense of identity in the communities of the Dispersion. The focus of Jewish worship, the Temple, was far away in Jerusalem, but his local synagogue was built to face in its direction. Here every week he came to gather with his fellow Jews around the scrolls of the *Torah*, the law which was the real bond that united all Jews everywhere. This was the holy rule of life God had given to his people, the focus of synagogue worship and the code which determined many details of daily life and custom. The ridicule heaped by outsiders upon many of its provisions, for instance on the rite of circumcision, only increased the fierceness of Jewish loyalty to it. It is to the rabbis of the communities of the Dispersion, especially in Mesopotamia at a somewhat later date, that we owe the most extensive collection of commentaries on the Law. Cultural osmosis and assimilation were not the only features of life in the Dispersion. Living 'in exile' from the Holy Land, among peoples to whom they always appeared as foreigners and among whom they instinctively felt themselves to be strangers, the Jews clung to the Holy Law as the core of their Jewish life and identity.

In their Palestinian homeland they were deeply divided over what kind of Jewish identity was implied by fidelity to the *Torah*. Since the days of Nehemiah and Ezra the Jews had learnt to regard themselves as a nation not only chosen by God but segregated from other nations by virtue of this choice. The divine code had to be observed meticulously to prevent their being merged among their gentile neighbours. The belief in their 'separateness' had brought the Jewish nation into sharp conflict with the Hellenistic world. The culture of that world had its appeal to many among the Jews; but many, also, felt the distinctive values of Judaism threatened by its spread. The ideological tension flared into conflict with the attempt by Antiochus IV to impose on the Jews the 'alien' culture. The crisis came when his desecration of the Temple in Jerusalem in 167 BC rallied the Jews against the pollution. The ensuing revolt, led by the family of the Maccabees, stamped the Jewish mentality with an intransigence in the face of foreign domination and suspicion of anything that might dilute the purity of Jewish life.

Roman supremacy in Palestine, whether exercised directly through Roman governors of Judaea or indirectly through local rulers such as Herod the Great (37–4 BC) created a complex political situation among the Jews. Religious, social and political divisions within the Jewish society into which Christianity was born reflect a variety of attitudes to the Roman power and the foreign culture. The Roman government had allowed a good deal of the High Priest's authority to survive; it was in the interests of the priestly aristocracy – the party of the Sadducees – to co-operate with the Roman authorities, and they adopted generally favourable attitudes towards the non-Jewish world. The chief opponents of their pro-Roman orientation at the time of Christ were the Pharisees. They were teachers of the *Torah* and enjoyed great prestige as a group devoted to the defence of God's Holy Law. They thought of themselves as the experts on all that made a Jew a Jew, and they were widely accepted as such. The Pharisees did not challenge the political power of Rome, so long as it could secure freedom for the Jews to continue living in fidelity to their ancestral traditions; it was in the detailed observance of these that they saw the whole substance of being a Jew. Even when, later on, the rabbis, especially in Mesopotamia, adopted a much wider liberalism in doctrine, they maintained this rigid conservatism on the observance of the Law.

There were other groups among whom a radical Jewish nationalism took a more fanatical form. Chief among these was the underground movement known as the 'Zealots', who acted as the mainspring of the insurrectionary movement against Roman rule during the first century AD. They were the bitterest opponents of foreign influence and of Jewish collaborators with it. Their political programme was sustained by a variety of apocalyptic hopes. In many Jewish circles there was a vivid sense of the scandal of the Holy Land under foreign power, and a belief in its deliverance by some mighty act of God. One such group organized itself as a religious community on the shores of the Dead Sea. Sometimes such expectations were centred on the coming of a saviour who would deliver God's people from the foreign yoke and establish the rule of God over them. There were all sorts of other groups, religious or political, of greater or lesser significance. In the New Testament we hear, for instance, of Herodians (Mark 12:13) and Hellenists (Acts 6:1).

One of these groups, that of the Nazarenes, received the name of 'Christians', apparently, for the first time at Antioch. The name was no doubt given them by outsiders to designate a distinctive grouping among the Jews. The group by now embraced some non-Jews, but as Judaism, too, had its proselytes, that would not be astonishing to anyone. The title would designate a group of Jews, followers of a man from Nazareth called Jesus, whom they believed to be the saviour ('Messiah' = 'Christos'). This Jesus had been suspect in the eyes of the Jewish authorities in Jerusalem and, on their denunciation, executed by the Roman government as a political agitator. Possibly he was suspected of being a Zealot or, less specifically, of being associated with a sect preaching apocalyptically inspired subversion. Some time around AD 30 he was executed in the company of two terrorists. Jesus had taken great care to distinguish his message from the nationalism of the Zealots; but the two were easily mistaken, and Jesus had as little success with some of his own followers as he had with the Roman authorities in convincing them that he had not come to liberate Israel from the Roman yoke. For all the world, his followers formed a movement among many others; the Jewish scene was pullulating with sects. Their leader, a Jew, like them, had moved and taught among Jews, like any rabbi. The disciples, naturally, also moved among their fellow Jews, preached the message of their master among them in the Temple and the synagogues; and it was their fellow Jews that their preaching divided.

Among the Jews the followers of Jesus were identifiable by their allegiance to him as their Lord; they were those who 'called upon his name'. We have an account of what they preached in a sermon placed in the mouth of Peter in Acts, 2: Jesus, a man singled out by God, through whom God had worked signs and portents, had been put to death; God raised him from the dead, exalted him and poured out his Spirit on the group gathered in his name. The time had come, the saviour promised by the prophets had appeared and the reign of God was at hand. His followers were the new Israel, grouped around the twelve leaders whom Jesus himself had chosen to be its 'foundation members'.

What in the first place distinguished this message from others more or less similar was the person on whom it was focussed. The saviour who both confounded many of the current expectations and answered their mood was believed

actually to have come in the person of Jesus. It was sometimes difficult, even for his disciples, to distinguish the liberation he offered from the sort of liberation others expected.
Instinctively they kept their distance from movements such
as that of the Zealots; it was not by subversion, or indeed
through any political action, that the promised kingdom
would come. But come it would, and soon. A new social
order in which God would rule his people in righteousness
would soon be visibly established among them. In the New
Testament it is possible to see both the survival of this firm
expectation, and the gradual extension of the time-scale on
which its consummation was expected. The return of the
Lord in glory to judge the world and to gather his faithful
into his Kingdom remained their permanent hope, but it was
becoming a hope fewer and fewer Christians expected to see
fulfilled very speedily. 'Come, Lord Jesus', was their prayer;
here and there apocalyptic expectations remained urgent,
and they were liable to revive sporadically for a long time yet,
but within two generations the Christian community was
learning to live in the world, prepared for a very long stay.

The core of their faith thus remained that the decisive act of
God in the establishing of his reign had been accomplished
in the career of Jesus. Everything else they derived from and
shared with either Judaism as a whole, or with one or other
of the crosscurrents within it. Their messianic expectations
were expressed in the language and the imagery of the Old
Testament prophetic writings and of Jewish apocalyptic
speculations. Their worship, rituals and common life had
parallels elsewhere, though in some cases it is not difficult to
exaggerate their closeness. They thought of themselves as the
'new Israel' of the Lord. The Old Testament was their sacred
book, indeed for a time their only 'scriptures'. Jewish worship
in the Temple and the synagogues was what they naturally
looked upon as the worship pleasing to the one true God, the
God of Abraham, Isaac and Jacob – and, now, the Father of
their Lord Jesus Christ. The outward form of Jewish life was
the immediately obvious form of living in accordance with

the commands God had given to his people. If they were a Jewish sect in the eyes of outsiders, they were the true Jews in their own.

The second instalment of Luke's account of Christian beginnings, The Acts of the Apostles, records not only the genesis of Christianity as a Jewish sect, but also the first stirrings and the rapid growth of the consciousness among the Christians that they were destined to become something else. Jesus' mission, to judge by the evidence of the synoptic Gospels, had been confined to 'the lost sheep of the house of Israel'. His disciples at first followed the example of their Lord in confining their activities within the Jewish orbit. There was a network of Jewish communities strung out along the Mediterranean coast; before long Christian missionaries were travelling around them, and we have no reason to assume that they did not also travel eastwards, as some later legends suggested. Missionary activity among gentiles was not without precedent in Judaism: the communities of the Dispersion provided the framework and perhaps also the model for the earliest Christian missions. The first Christians to detach the Gospel from the Jewish cult were probably members of a dissident Jewish group, with strong Hellenistic sympathies and heterodox views on Jewish temple worship. They had turned to Christianity in Jerusalem and dispersed when their leader, Stephen, was lynched by a Jewish mob. At first even they preached the Gospel only among Jews, until some of them, in line with the inner logic of their attitude, took the momentous step in the great Hellenistic city of Antioch of 'preaching the Lord Jesus to Greeks also' (Acts 11:20).

Their gentile converts were taken under the wing of the 'official' apostolic mission, based on Jerusalem. Peter, pre-eminent among the twelve, was drawn into the gentile mission, and Paul, a convert Pharisee, to whom Stephen and the 'Hellenists' had been especially obnoxious, threw himself into this work and soon dominated it. But it took the Christian community in Jerusalem some time to overcome its hesitations, and its leaders for long remained divided over the policy to be adopted in regard to gentile converts to Christianity. Behind the uncertainties concerning the extent to which such converts should be expected to observe the Jewish Law we can easily discern the fundamental uncertainty: was Christianity a way of being a Jew or was it something else? Despite agreed compromises, tensions between the universalists, that is, those who worked beyond the Jewish social and cultural context, and the more conservative Jewish Christians long continued. For nearly four centuries groups survived which conceived Christianity in Jewish terms; they were recruited largely – though not entirely – among Jews, and their horizons remained those of Judaism. Augustine of Hippo, around 400, was still acquainted with such a group; and some of them even undertook extensive propaganda, for instance in the Near East. In North Africa, the Christian Church seems to have kept links with the synagogues for a very long time. But from about the middle of the second century such Jewish Christian groups were beginning to be regarded by most Christians as deviant or even heretical. The fall of Jerusalem in the war that followed the Jewish insurrection (66–70) gave Christian universalism a great boost. The destruction of the Temple and the dissolution of the Jewish community forced the Christians to emerge into independent existence. Increasingly the social life of the Christian Church, the forms of religious observance, of thought and culture, developed outside the Jewish milieu. Early in the second century Ignatius, Bishop of Antioch, contrasts 'Christianism' with 'Judaism'. The sections of the Church which clung to the outlook of the original Jerusalem community – to which some forms of Jewish Christianity appear to be traceable – became increasingly anomalous in the 'great Church' as it spread through the gentile world. The lines were becoming clearly drawn between a universal Church and a Judaism identified, after 70, with the Pharisaic tradition perpetuated in rabbinic Judaism.

In the second century the destinies of Christianity and Judaism were diverging visibly. In the fourth century, the Church's triumph was to set the seal upon a division which had hardened into hostility. In John Chrysostom's sermons preached in Antioch in 387 we can catch a note of the same hysterical denigration, now turned by a Christian against Jews, which in an earlier age had been a feature of some of the more obscene accusations made by pagans against Christians. Almost from the first moment of the Church's newly won toleration, Jews began to feel the repressive edge of imperial legislation, and before the end of the century a Christian bishop, Ambrose of Milan, was to browbeat an emperor into denying the Jews the ordinary protection afforded by the law to all Roman subjects. The ugly forces of Christian anti-semitism and mob violence could combine, as in Alexandria in 413, when the Jews were expelled from the city. Theologians, far from recognizing common ground with the Jews in the Old Testament, were busy with reinterpretation: it was the heritage of the new Israel, in which the Israel after the flesh was to have no rights.

The long sad story of Christian anti-semitism had scarcely as yet begun in the second century. In the course of it, however, Christianity was acquiring an identity clearly separate from Judaism. In the eyes of outsiders as well as in their own, Christians were becoming a distinct group. They were the people who rejected both the gods of the Greeks and the superstitions of the Jews, as a Christian writer put it.[3] Alongside the Jews and the gentiles they were a new people, a 'third race' (or, if Greeks and barbarians were enumerated separately, as they sometimes were, a 'fourth').[4]

CHAPTER TWO

The third race

THE ROMAN HISTORIAN Livy has a story[1] about a religious movement which was considered a menace to society. It is described as a 'second people'. The pagans who in the second and third centuries referred to Christians as the 'third people' or the 'third race' saw them as something alien and suspect, potentially sinister. 'Away with the third race' was a favourite shout of the crowds in the circus.[2] The phrase neatly pinpointed the recognizable identity that Christians were acquiring, distinct from both Jews and pagans. No such designation could have taken root unless Christians had in fact developed a distinct corporate identity, even a separateness, in the society around them. Christians sometimes also used the phrase in reference to themselves, as if to stress their own emerging coherence.

Their communities incurred the suspicions that cliquish minorities commonly arouse. Rumours of secret crimes at Christian religious celebrations gained easy currency. Nero had found that the 'notoriously depraved Christians' made convenient scapegoats for the great fire in Rome (64). Tacitus, reporting the incident, though no lover of Nero, shared this estimate: in his eyes, too, Christianity was a 'deadly superstition'.[3] Secret abominations long continued to be associated with the Christian name; in the second century the official trial of Christians 'for the name' (i.e., on the charge of being Christians) could easily be associated with charges of secret crime. Calumny fed popular indignation; and this often provided the occasion for official proceedings against Christians. To a pagan opponent late in the second century, the educated and well-informed Celsus, Christians seemed as people who 'wall themselves off and break away from the rest of mankind'.[4] Even in the following century they were described as a 'lurking breed which avoids the light of day'.[5] They were subject to the unpopularity that was often the fate of the Jews; but the unpopularity was compounded with suspicion and fear born of bafflement. The 'third race', in separating itself from its Jewish milieu, had lost the benefit of antiquity, which alone had made the Jews traditionally acceptable in the Roman world.

Christian apologists in the second century sometimes seem to take pride in the hatred of outsiders. All the evidence, both from inside and outside the Christian groups, suggests that they had become noticeable as a close-knit, inward-looking minority generally does. Members of the group felt themselves bound together by an intimacy which struck outsiders. Pagans thought the intimacy was forged only by a common danger – an account Christians energetically denied.[6] They had good grounds for their denial. 'Look how these Christians love one another' was not always said in irony. In the Christian community of a large Roman city the rootless and the uprooted, the newly arrived and the lonely could find a group to which they could belong. They would find mutual support, for the brotherhood provided for its members as complete a system of social security as could be found in the ancient world. And more – they would find a human warmth and closeness in which their need to belong could receive real satisfaction.

Cliques often generate private conventions, habits of language and of behaviour characteristic of the group. From quite early in its history, Christianity generated its own idiom. This process left much less of a mark on the Greek spoken in Christian circles than it left, somewhat later, on the Latin current among them. Greek was the language in which the Gospel had been first proclaimed outside Palestine. It was the international form of the Hellenistic 'common tongue', the universal language of travellers and displaced persons over much of the Roman world. Christians naturally used it, and their version evolved its own peculiarities. Above all, as used by Christians, it bore the deep imprint of Hellenistic Jewish tradition, being saturated with the usages and rhythms of the Alexandrian version of the Old Testament. The emergence of a Christian Latin language in Rome and Africa in the course of the second century was less discreet. Perhaps Christians here were less subject to the restraining force of literary tradition. In any case, to meet the requirements of their worship and their theology the less subtle, less flexible and less rich Latin language needed more transformation. Christian Latin came to abound with borrowings from the Greek, with neologisms and solecisms. It is a language at once exotic and popular, mirroring the experience of group-solidarity. The linguistic evolution shows the crystallization of a self-conscious Christian group with its distinctive sub-culture. The literature produced by Christians was for the most part intended to be read by Christians, and even what was written for outsiders seems to have circulated largely within the group. Curiously, even the form they chose for their books marked them off from others. Instead of the ubiquitous roll, used in Greek and Jewish circles alike, they showed a distinct preference for the codex form, two centuries or more before the Greco-Roman world at large came to share this preference. For their holy book, the Bible, the preference amounted to almost exclusive choice, tantalizing in its uniformity in an age when Christian communities had little organization and no common authority.

The 'third race' had certainly emerged into a very distinct existence, forming a recognizable Christian sub-culture, discernible to members of the group and outsiders alike, in the course of the second century. In the last chapter we saw how the Christians' consciousness of being the 'new Israel' set them aside from the Jews. That was an untidy development, with many hesitations and uncertainties. We come now to consider the much longer and more tangled process whereby the Christian community defined itself in relation to the pagan world. In the present chapter we shall consider only the first stages of this process, the period during the second and third centuries, when Christianity remained a minority religion. As a milieu in which Christianity took shape, the pagan world did not, of course, possess even the sort of coherence that Judaism possessed – not only because it was a larger and more varied world, but even more because paganism was not a religion, at least not in the sense that Judaism and Christianity were 'religions'. In this sense paganism became a religion only very late, in the later third century and the fourth, and it was a product of Christianity. Paganism as a religion took shape in contrast with its rival, Christianity, and in conscious opposition to it. For Christians, religion was a matter of the worship, of the beliefs and of the standards of conduct shared by the members of the community. In the Greco-Roman world there was a wide variety of religious movements, cults and schools of philosophy. But they catered for different needs, and overlapped only in part with what the Christian Church provided for its members. The scholar who came to know this world best, the late A. D. Nock, has summed up the difference thus: 'The Jew and the Christian offered religions as we understand religion; the others offered cults; but their contemporaries did not expect anything more than cults from them and looked to philosophy for guidance in conduct and for a scheme of the Universe. . . . Worship had no key to life's meaning: that was offered by philosophy . . .'.[7] Christianity offered its adherents both a cult and a philosophy. It gave a key to the meaning of life and provided a rule for its conduct as well as a worship in the Spirit and the truth.

As a cult, Christianity set itself in uncompromising opposition to all other cults. From Judaism it inherited the fear of a jealous God who would brook no worship of other gods. A second-century Roman provincial governor knew very well that Christians could not, even on pain of death, be made so much as to go through the motions of offering wine or incense before a statue of the emperor.[8] By their inflexible

27

intolerance of other cults, Christians set themselves at odds with the 'peace of the gods'; they repudiated the harmonious relationship between gods and men and damaged the peaceful co-existence of public religion and private cults.

In the classical world, public cults had been essentially a local and civic affair. The existence of a number of gods, and the rivalry of foreign deities seldom caused conflict. In the course of conquest and of the extension of Greek culture, foreign deities were sometimes equated with, sometimes assimilated to, one or other Greek deity. In the Roman Empire, too, native gods tended to travel to Rome and often to assume Roman guise and to mingle with the Capitoline deities, sometimes despite the resistance of conservatives. Although particular cults were sometimes regarded as outlandish curiosities, or despised as foreign superstitions, cults were not generally thought to be in competition. Symmachus, one of the last spokesmen of Roman paganism, writing at the end of the fourth century, summed up the traditional pagan attitude: 'Not by one way alone do we arrive at so great a secret.'

On the meticulous discharge of men's duties towards their gods was thought to depend the safety and prosperity of the community. Symmachus, again, was only voicing the traditional belief when he attributed Rome's victories and conquests to the exact performance of her duties to the gods. Although Christians rejected all pagan cults without compromise, and incurred hatred, hostility and reprisal in consequence, they often shared the fundamentals of the pagan belief that impiety could bring down the wrath of the deity on the whole community. The Emperor Constantine plainly thought that the Empire might suffer from God's displeasure if he, as a Christian emperor, failed to carry out the divine will. Something like the same assumption appears to underlie the argument occasionally used by Christian apologists that good emperors – those who have been tolerant towards Christianity – have been rewarded by God with victory, success and other signs of His favour and the bad punished by trouble in the Empire. Melito of Sardis related the flourishing of the Roman Empire since its foundation by Augustus to the excellence of the Christian religion established during his reign. His approach provided the basis for an interpretation of Christianity as the imperial religion; it could be represented as replacing the multitude of cults of the warring cities and nations by the universal cult of the one, universal empire. This line of thought had a great future in store in the theology of the christianized Empire of the fourth century.

Thus rejection of all cults as idolatrous did not prevent Christians from sharing some of the assumptions current about the purpose of religious cults. This is also true of the more personal cults and mystery religions, with many of which Christianity shared a basic purpose as well as common assumptions about the world, human and divine. If Alfred North Whitehead's dictum that religion is what a man does with his solitude has any truth, it is in the sphere of these cults. Here a man looked for deliverance from the absurdity of his life in this world, for a promise of salvation in another world, for a revelation of the divine and a ritual union with it. The longing for deliverance was common to pagans and Christians who could speak in much the same language about the insignificance or the unreality of life on this earth or the horror of the human condition. Men were not 'at home in the body' and found any identification with their world impossible. It had to be rejected as vile, treated as a joke or accepted with resignation as a place of trial; in whatever way the world of space and time was explained, men felt themselves, in their innermost being, to belong elsewhere.

There were, of course, some pagan and, exceptionally, Christian thinkers who found it possible to achieve a measure of harmonious equilibrium in the world, to praise it and to feel at home in it. There is a risk of over-estimating the otherworldliness of late antiquity; in this period, as in many others, the articulate expression of religious feelings may be by no means representative of more than small minorities. But even at the risk of allowing the articulate more than a fair weight, the innumerable religions which opposed a world of light to a world of darkness, or a world of spirit to a world of matter, were, somehow, closer to the instincts of men from the late second century onwards. The projection of inner conflicts on to the stage of the outer world was the mainspring of the dualistic religions of late antiquity; they opposed two worlds, each in the grip of one or other of the warring powers of a good and an evil ultimate principle. The world was the theatre of their conflict, and man was caught up in it until his final release and return to his true home. The cosmology of the two worlds and the imagery of man's destiny in them distilled the sense of alienation and revulsion on which their strong appeal rested.

Christianity as well as pagan philosophy could provide antidotes to these feelings of revulsion (see below, p. 38). Christians could not accept the cosmological dualism which would amount to a denial of one, good, all-creating God. Nevertheless, they did to a large extent share the pessimistic response to the world for which dualistic religions were the vehicles. From Judaism Christianity inherited a rich vocabulary of exile; it was put to good use to express the widely felt alienation. In the words of an anonymous Christian writer around 200, Christians 'dwell in their own countries, but only as sojourners; they bear their share in all things as citizens, and they endure all hardships as strangers. Every foreign country is a fatherland to them, and every fatherland foreign. . . . Their existence is on earth, their citizenship in heaven.'[9] In this by no means uncharacteristic statement of Christian alienation the words of the Bible blend unobtrusively with the commonplaces of Hellenistic thought. The commonplaces were given new life in neo-Platonic philosophy. Plotinus (*c.* 205–70), patronized by Roman aristocrats under the Emperor Gallienus, asked in a similar vein: 'Why should the wise man think that falling from power and the ruin of his city are great matters?'[10] – a question Augustine of Hippo was to quote as he lay dying. In all his earthly sojourn man was journeying towards his homeland, carried by ardent longing, like Odysseus returning from the Trojan wars, through danger and privation, through the terror of the clashing rocks and past the seductive song of the Sirens. Plotinus quoted Homer's 'Let us fly to our dear country';[11] for him, as for countless Christians, Odysseus was a symbol of man on his journey through the world. Christians were committed to the belief that the pain and suffering of the world were bound up with a primal fall from grace. Some of them went further and toyed with the notion – a notion which also had wide currency among non-Christians – that the fall had been a fall into the body. Resentment against the world was easily concentrated in resentment of self imprisoned in a body. For many Christians, as for many pagans, the body became the chief locus of all the frustrating powers of the world. The abuse heaped upon the flesh and the asceticism that flowed from such attitudes were no monopoly of Christianity, even though they long continued to infect Christian attitudes; nor, for that matter, was occasional protest and reassertion of the goodness of all material creation.

In the sphere of sex and marriage, however, Christian asceticism outstripped the most negative of pagan attitudes. The Christian editor of a pagan handbook of moral precepts, rigorous as was the original, felt he had to improve on it. In his reworking we read that marriage and the begetting of children is the worst possible thing for the man who wishes to cleave to God; if he must marry, let his marriage be a competition in continence with his wife.[12] There were rare Christians, such as the Egyptian Bishop Paphnutius, who had suffered in the persecution of Diocletian. At the Council of Nicaea (325) he defended the married state as honourable among all and 'called a man's intercourse with his lawful wife chastity'.[13] The generally prevalent view, however, was that a Christian was permitted to marry only for the sake of procreating and bringing up children and was otherwise to remain continent. This view, too, was widely current among pagan moralists.[14] Asceticism was not unknown in either the

(Continued on p. 38)

1 Felicitas temporis, panel from Altar of Augustan Peace, Rome, 13–9 BC.

Ancient fidelity and peace, honour, modesty and forgotten virtue now return once more, and blessed plenty with a full horn
HORACE, *Carmen saeculare*, 56f.
see page 13

2 Ezra, the scribe, from Codex Amiatinus, AD 715. Biblioteca Laurenziana, Florence.

. . . all the words of this law: it is not a trivial matter for you, for it is your life
Deuteronomy, 32.47.
see page 17

GOD'S CHOSEN PEOPLE UNDER THE ROMAN YOKE

3 Judaea capta, coin of Titus, *c.* AD 70. British Museum, London.

4 Spoils of the temple, Jerusalem, panel from Arch of Titus, Rome, AD 81.

Behold our sanctuary and our beauty and our glory is laid waste and the gentiles have defiled them
I Maccabees, 2.12.
see page 17

5 Graffito depicting a crucified donkey, from Palatine Antiquarium, *c.* AD 200. Museo Nazionale delle Terme, Rome.

Who is so stupid that he should believe this to be an object of worship?
MINUCIUS FELIX, *Octavius*, 28.7.

but rumours that Christians worshipped an ass's head circulated freely.
see page 24

6 The brotherhood meal, detail of Baebia Hertofile sarcophagus, late 3rd century. Museo Nazionale delle Terme, Rome.   see page 25

2

3

4

5

6

7

8

9

10

11

7 The Holy Book: Codex Sinaiticus (before binding), 4th century. British Museum, London.

see page 26

8 Odysseus and the sirens, detail of sarcophagus of Aurelius Romanus, 3rd century. Museo Nazionale delle Terme, Rome.

Let us flee from worldliness . . . as Odysseus fled from the Sirens in the story: for by it is a man suffocated, seduced from the truth, brought even to his death
CLEMENT OF ALEXANDRIA, *Protrepticus*, xii.12.

Odysseus as a symbol of man's journey to his true home was used by Pagans and Christians alike.

see page 31

9 Christ the Victor represented in the military garb of an imperator trampling on a lion and a serpent, mosaic in Archiepiscopal Chapel, Ravenna, 6th century (restored).
In the tabernacle of the flesh Christ the imperator has done battle for us
AUGUSTINE, *Enarrationes in Psalmum* XC, *sermo* ii.5.

see page 38

THE EDUCATED MAN AS AN IDEAL TYPE

10 Philosopher surrounded by disciples, detail of sarcophagus, 3rd century. Musei Vaticani (Lateran), Rome.
the soul on its way to Hades takes nothing with it but its nurture and education
PLATO, *Phaedo* 107D.

11 Christ as the supreme educator and the Gospels as the true philosophy, detail of ivory casket, 4th century. Museo Civico, Brescia.

see pages 39–41

pagan or the Jewish world; the shifts in men's attitudes to their own bodies, especially from the late second century onwards, intensified their instinctive recoil from the flesh. Christians were not immune to the neuroses of their contemporaries. If anything, they were liable to experience them in a heightened degree.

Pagan philosophy and Christian belief could both offer ways of integrating the material world in a good and beautiful universe. For Plotinus the world of matter, though from one viewpoint it was the principle of evil, could also be looked upon as a graded hierarchy of reflections of the highest realities. Repudiating gnostic dualism as blasphemous, he asserted that the material world is 'a clear and noble image of the intelligible gods' and that its beauty leads men to the contemplation of the supreme realities. It was with the aid of Plotinus' metaphysics that Augustine of Hippo, converted from Manichaean dualism, would find a way of reconciling evil with the goodness of a universe created by an all-powerful and perfectly good God. But Christians also had resources for overcoming their estrangement from the body and matter, resources not available to others. Christ, they knew, had conquered the demons and defeated their power over the material creation. They were still active, but on a short leash; men could now hope to conquer them in the name of Christ and with his aid; and the days of their dominion were, in any case, numbered. Baptism had snatched the Christian from their power and their bankruptcy had only to be made visible for all to see by displaying the power of Christ triumphing over the power of the devil.

The Christian cult, then, aimed to meet needs similar to those which other cults claimed to satisfy. Initiation into the mysteries offered more than satisfaction of curiosity about the hereafter: it gave assurance of salvation in an inhospitable world. What Christian ritual, especially sacramental practice and symbolism, owed to the mystery religions is probably not a very great deal. But it sprang from the same longing of men for liberation from the rack of a world on to which they projected similar images of conflict and frustration. For anxious men seeking to come to terms with themselves and their fate, Christianity would have offered one among several possible answers. It preached reconciliation with God through Jesus and promised salvation to those who believed in him. The cult in which it gave access to the reconciliation effected by Christ differed in a crucial way from other systems of religious worship. To be a Christian meant more than being initiated into a religious group and participating in its ritual observances. Therein lay the reason for the resolute refusal of Christians to participate in the Roman cults; for them, their own cult could never be what cults were for others, mere ritual acts. There was also a question of truth involved.

In the ancient world such questions were generally thought to be the concern of philosophy rather than of religion. Among the Greeks speculative thinking had crystallized out of mythological thinking very early, and became an alternative approach to the divine. If philosophy and cult were distinct, we must be careful, however, not to press their distinctness too far. Philosophic and religious concerns converged in two ways. First, in the period with which we are dealing the speculative and analytical thinking which we associate with 'philosophy' was becoming widely fossilized into schools with a dogmatic tradition. There were, of course, genuine philosophic thinkers and creative work long continued to be done in Athens and Alexandria. But outside the schoolroom, and to some extent also inside it, to be a philosopher of the Stoic, or the Platonic or any other school could mean no more than adhering to a body of doctrines compendiously codified. Secondly, even on the level at which philosophy was pursued by creative thinkers like Plotinus, the goals of philosophy were akin to those of religion. Men looked to philosophy for an explanatory scheme of the world, of man and of God. And in catering for this longing, philosophy came increasingly to mean the quest of God. Its activity might culminate in a union or a vision which we might be tempted to call 'mystical'. Moreover, in the Greco-Roman world philosophy was often seen as a way of life. The Pythagorean philosophical school, for example, resembled a religious order with a detailed rule of life which included quite specific detail such as abstinence from beans. The philosophic life in general was held to imply a break with the accepted norms of conduct; asceticism, self-denial and renunciation of worldliness went with it. The image of the philosopher is one of the ideal types venerated in antiquity and provided Christianity with a type for the saint. Conversion to philosophy was perhaps the nearest the ancient world came to approaching the idea of conversion to Christianity.

Christianity, therefore, was more than a cult; it would have been seen as a philosophy as well. It introduced its adherents not only into a cult and a cult-community, but at the same time into a 'school' with its own vision of the saving truth about God, man and the world, and with a scheme of life which showed them the posture appropriate to man in this world. Christians were aware that cult and philosophy were uniquely combined in their religion. Quite regularly in the second and third centuries Christianity is in fact referred to as a 'philosophy'. Pagan scholars resented the claim, for it enabled Christians to short-cut the discipline of thought and learning by an appeal to a revelation; but Christians were undeterred by the protest. Justin Martyr (*c.* 100–*c.* 165), for instance, tells his readers [15] that he ended up as a Christian, having made trial of all the philosophical schools. His story may be a series of anti-philosophical commonplaces clothed in the forms of autobiography, but it reveals his approach to Christianity. His teachers, he says, all failed him: the Stoic could not advance his knowledge of God; the Peripatetic asked him for money, thereby revealing himself to be no true philosopher; the Pythagorean insisted on his equipping himself in all the preparatory disciplines, music, astronomy and geometry; even Platonism disappointed him in his hopes of being taught the way to the vision of God. A chance meeting with an old man convinced him that the truth about God is not to be sought from philosophers but from the prophets, who spoke in the divine spirit. Hearing him, Justin concludes, 'I conceived an ardent love for the prophets and those men who are Christ's friends; and pondering on his words I discovered that only this one philosophy was safe and profitable. Thus, and for this reason, I am a philosopher.'[16]

To a man of Justin's expectations from philosophy, Christianity was a philosophy. Christians were aware that their religion offered a synthesis of what was generally two separate things in the ancient world. Augustine of Hippo at the end of the fourth century, comparing paganism and Christianity, thought that Christianity alone had brought a resolution of the ancient tensions between cult and philosophy.[17] In this he was nearly right. Pagan philosophy had often been very cool towards popular religion. For the educated pagan the popular cults were often no more than clumsy means of embodying the truths of philosophy on a level accessible to the common run of men. Religious traditions could be read as allegories of the hidden truth uncovered by the learned. And the truth when seen in this sort of way took on an increasingly monotheistic hue. Pagan thought had also found ways of integrating religious cult in philosophic monotheism. Indeed, by the middle of the third century, polytheism had long ago ceased to be a serious rival to Christianity. There is an air of artificiality about the set debates between Christians and pagans concerning the gods. Thoughtful pagans had long been transposing the myths about their gods into a more sophisticated and essentially monotheistic key. Christian monotheism, on the other hand, was very hospitable to a large variety of beings intermediate between God and men. In the second and third centuries it is sometimes a nice question to decide whether a particular pagan or Christian writer presents a stricter monotheism. A pagan correspondent, holder of pagan priesthoods, wrote to Augustine thus: 'There is a better way to God by which a good man hastens to travel by piety, purity, justice, chastity and truth in his words and in his deeds, unmoved by the vicissitudes of changeful times and guarded by the company of gods – that is, by the powers of God, filled with the strength of the one universal, incomprehensible, ineffable and unwearied Creator: I believe you call them angels. . . .'[18] It is not immediately obvious that such monotheism is less strict than many versions of Christian monotheism.

As early as the middle of the second century there were educated Christians who were beginning to be conscious of the relative narrowness of the gap which divided their beliefs from those current among their educated pagan friends and colleagues. They could not remain content with an image of Christianity which represented it as something wholly alien to the pagan world. Justin, for example, represented Christianity as summing up all that was best in the thought of antiquity. Platonism, in particular, he thought, had anticipated some of the central truths of Christian belief. One way of accounting for such evidences of the Gospel before Christ was a well-tried way of Hellenistic Jewish apologetics: Plato and the early Greek thinkers who had stumbled upon the truth had found it, in a thinly veiled form, in the prophetic utterances of Moses; or, Plato had learnt these central truths on his journeys to Egypt, in the course of which he met Jeremiah. (Hence much ink was spilt in proving the priority of the Pentateuch or of the Hebrew prophets to the Greek thinkers.) Several Christian apologists, including Justin, adopted such an explanation for the 'borrowings' of sacred truth by Plato and Homer. This sort of explanation long continued in vogue, but it was an expedient of popular apologetics rather than a serious attempt to take the measure of Greek philosophy in relation to Christian faith. Justin was not content to leave the matter at that. He perceived a more fundamental relationship between Christianity and the previous achievements of the human intellect, especially in Greek thought. He expressed this relationship in the language of Stoic philosophy: the world was permeated through and through by a cosmic reason *(logos)*. All those who, before

Christ, had lived 'with the *logos*' lived well and in accordance
with the truth. The *logos* disseminated among all men enabled
some of them to glimpse the truth for themselves. What they
perceived in a fragmentary way from afar has been revealed
in its fullness to all in Christ, the Word *(Logos)* made flesh.
All positive achievement before Christ could thus be understood as part of his truth, and Christianity as the rounding off
and completion of men's previous groping approaches to the
truth. Greek philosophy, especially, was a preparation for the
Gospel. A Christian could listen to the *logos* and should be
prepared to find truth anywhere.

Justin's was the first serious attempt in the history of
Christian thought to find a way of relating Christian belief
with the thought of the Greco-Roman world. That something less arbitrary and jejune than the hypothesis of Greek
plagiarism from the Jews was needed would in any case have
become clear before long. The Christian group had come
into being preaching a simple message, consisting of certain
facts about Jesus; facts that the Jews, and soon all men, should
know. The preaching of this message around the Hellenistic
cities of the Mediterranean basin faced them with the need to
make it comprehensible not only to Jews. The message
would have to be translated into the categories in which their
audience were accustomed to think. Moreover, educated
men were beginning to be found – despite the jibes of
pagans – in the ranks of the Christians. Inevitably such men
would ask themselves how the intellectual equipment they
had brought with them from their pagan education could
find a place, even perhaps a useful function, within the
Christian Church. The need for an intellectual and cultural
bridge was clear and urgent by the end of the second century.

Justin's attempt to find such a bridge had been, in a way,
hinted at by the writer of The Acts of the Apostles (ch. 17)
in the speech he placed in the mouth of St Paul on the
occasion of a visit to Athens. Taking his cue from the sight
of an altar to 'the unknown god', Paul is made to preach his
god as the one for whom his Greek audience had been

groping in the dark. Christianity is the answer to their search and reveals the object of their mute worship. This could be taken as apostolic warrant for a cultural integration of Christianity in the thought-world of Hellenism.

It was not till late in the second century that any sustained attempt to achieve such an integration was made. The Christian group remained confined within the intellectual horizons of Judaism long after it had in fact acquired an existence distinct from Judaism. Judaism was not, of course, a closed world without contacts with Hellenistic culture. Christianity must have found the Hellenized Jewish communities of the Dispersion its earliest catchment area and the most promising springboard for a wider mission. Christian preachers may well have come to share something of the Hellenized culture which they must have found among such Jews. But in the eyes of outsiders Judaism was a form of barbarism; that is, quite simply, it did not belong to the sphere of Greek (or later, Roman) civilization. Christianity naturally inherited the barbarism of its progenitor. Even late in the second century it was seen as 'a doctrine originally barbarian'.[19] But it was seen thus not only by pagan outsiders. Tatian, a Syrian who became, as it happens, a pupil of Justin in Rome and turned to Christianity, could write in scathing terms about 'your [i.e., Greek] philosophers'.[20] His total response to classical civilization was sharply opposed to Justin's: he readily identified himself with 'barbarism' and took glory in the 'barbarity' of Christianity.[21] Even men as little inclined to oppose Christianity and Hellenism as Justin and Clement of Alexandria (see below, pp. 46–47) sometimes adopted this language, in which Christianity (and Judaism) were forms of barbarism. Late in the third century the pagan Porphyry used the same language to censure the conversion of the great Alexandrian scholar Origen to Christianity: 'A Greek educated in Greek thought, he plunged headlong into the barbarian recklessness.'[22] Pagan polemic long continued to make use of this commonplace. Its opponents were only too ready to draw a sharp line around Christianity and to define it as alien to Greco-Roman culture. Christians, even when they struggled to free themselves from this manner of seeing themselves, found the very language an obstacle. If their emancipation from Judaism exposed them to persecution, their residual association with it was enough, in the eyes of pagans, to oppose them to Greco-Roman culture as barbarians. It was an image of exclusion difficult to discard; the very language, saturated in centuries of Greek convictions of superiority, stamped the Christians as outsiders.

Some, like Tatian (and others whom we shall consider in the next chapter), were very ready to consider themselves as outsiders. The Gospel had after all been preached as foolishness to the Greeks, and there were good reasons why Christians as well as pagans should be reminded of the fact. But almost from the earliest times this cast of mind was one of two opposed attitudes current among Christians. Not much survives of the Christian apologetic literature of the second century. Most of what does survive represents the current opposed to Tatian's views. Its aim is not only to dispel the grosser calumnies and the charges of political disloyalty, but to represent Christianity as acceptable by the sort of standards, both of thought and of conduct, to which the ordinary educated Greco-Roman citizen would assent. But the apologists only sketched a programme. The programme was to be carried out at Alexandria. It was there, from the end of the second century onwards, that the first wide-ranging syntheses of Christianity and Greek culture were being carried out.

Alexandria had been one of the greatest centres of learning in the Hellenistic world. Here Judaism had gone farthest in assimilating the culture of the Greek world. The Christian Church in Alexandria inherited this openness to the cultural environment. Its origins in Alexandria are entirely obscure. The Church must have entered an exceptionally active scene with Jews, Jewish Christians of various degrees of heterodoxy, and an assortment of gnostic heresies (see next chapter) and a thriving pagan culture which must have flourished alongside the episcopal church. This, in comparison with the intellectual ferment around it, would have seemed unexciting, if not rigidly obscurantist. Towards the end of the century, however, a Christian school emerged as its adjunct under one Pantaenus, a widely travelled and cultured philosopher convert. His pupil, Clement, who succeeded him as master of the school, must rank as the first Christian writer to carry out the programme sketched by the second-century apologists.

Clement followed out the hint given in the sermon attributed to St Paul in Acts; he saw Christianity as the fulfilment of the highest hopes of the pre-Christian world. Just as the Law had been the Jews' 'schoolmaster . . . unto Christ' (Gal. 3:24), so philosophy prepared the Greeks for the Gospel. Clement's endorsement of Greek philosophy epitomizes his whole estimate of the secular culture of his time. 'The earth is the Lord's and the fulness thereof,' he quoted once, and went on: 'and anyone who wants to help catechumens, especially if they be Greeks, must not shrink from scholarly study.'[23] His treatment of the problems of Christian conduct is an attempt to provide Christians with a sane and balanced rule for living in the world, not set apart from it. He did not repudiate asceticism, but he was reserved about it, and thought of it as a special calling akin to that of the martyr. Far from advocating asceticism as the norm of behaviour for the ordinary Christian, Clement devoted a whole treatise to showing that even a rich man could be saved. He conceived the Christian life as one of reasonable self-restraint and discipline, and the Christian community as one which had a place for many different levels and kinds of holiness. His was a Christian code of ethics for the reasonable man, such as an educated Alexandrian might be.

His successor in the Alexandrian school, Origen, had a greater ascetic temperament and he was apt to take a more austere view of pagan society and its values. But in one respect his mind was more receptive than Clement's towards pagan culture. He was very much at home in the world of philosophic argumentation and he assimilated a great deal of Greek philosophy, especially of Platonic inspiration, into his own thinking. Clement and Origen, who had both shown that it was possible for the scholar to find a home in the Christian Church, between them charted a course which led it, in the end, into the heritage of classical civilization. But there were other courses open, some diametrically opposed to theirs, and for a long time yet a Christianity conceived in their style met severe hostility and competition in the church.

A pupil of Origen, Gregory the Wonderworker, wrote, recalling the education he had received from his beloved master: 'No subject was forbidden us; nothing was hidden or inaccessible. We were encouraged to become acquainted with every doctrine, barbarian or Greek, with things spiritual and secular, divine and human, ranging with all freedom and confidence through the whole realm of knowledge, refreshing ourselves with the enjoyment of all the good things of the mind.'[24] 'He [Origen] said – rightly – that no one could practise true piety without philosophizing.'[25]

While Clement, Origen and their pupils had a lively sense that the whole range of the treasure accumulated by antiquity was theirs to be used and enjoyed, a very different tradition, with equally venerable credentials, found voice elsewhere.

CHAPTER THREE

The crisis of identity

OPTIMISM is a by-product of self-confidence. The optimism distinctive of Alexandrian Christianity was based on the belief that everything that was best in the world pointed to Christianity and found a home in the Church. Men like Justin, Clement and Origen, and for that matter Philo before them, saw no radical discontinuity between the culture of classical antiquity and Judaism or Christianity. They had the self-confidence to set about the task of integrating their sympathies with the world of classical antiquity into their religious commitment. They saw no threat here to their Christian identity. Assimilating Greek thought and learning did not appear to them as likely to submerge their Christian faith beneath a culture felt to be alien or hostile. But there were Christian thinkers who profoundly distrusted the kind of intellectual accommodation between Christanity and secular culture towards which Justin, Clement and Origen were pointing. What gave force to this current of opposition to their conception of Christianity in the second and third centuries?

St Paul had drawn the contrast in the sharpest possible way between the wisdom of this world, which is foolishness with God, and the foolishness of God which is wiser than men (1 Cor. 1:18–25). There were many Christians in the second and third centuries to whom St Paul's warning remained an urgent reminder of the gulf between the world and the Gospel of Jesus Christ, through whom alone it has pleased God to save those who believe. We have seen that Tatian rejected the wisdom of the Greeks in the name of the 'barbarity' of the Gospel. He was not alone; and in the third century the onslaught against classical culture was given a new intensity by Origen's older contemporary, the African Tertullian (*c.* 170–220).

Tertullian gave this consciousness of a radical discontinuity between Christianity and all secular thought and culture the most trenchant expression. 'What is there in common between the philosopher and the Christian?', he asked in a famous series of passionate rhetorical questions; 'what between the disciple of Greece and the disciple of heaven? . . . the friend and the enemy of error?'[1] Worldly wisdom is a rash interpreter of the divine nature and dispensation; philosophy and heresy are akin: 'What has Athens to do with Jerusalem? the Academy with the Church? heresy with Christianity?' We must seek the Lord in simplicity of heart. Away with all projects for a 'Stoic' or a 'platonic' or a 'dialectical' Christianity. 'After Jesus Christ we have no more scope for further curiosity, after the Gospel no need for further research.'[2] And if anyone were to quote the Lord's command 'seek, and ye shall find; knock, and it shall be opened unto you' (Matt. 7:7–8), Tertullian had his answer: these commands had been addressed by Jesus to the Jews early in his ministry, before they could have known that he was the Messiah. But for us, his followers, who have accepted him as the saviour and to whom the Paraclete has been promised to lead us into all truth, the saying 'has lost its relevance'.[3] And if one insists on taking it as addressed to all men, what it means, Tertullian suggests, is this: 'Seek until you find and believe when you have found; seek no more except to guard what you believe, believing in addition only that nothing else is to be either believed or sought after when you have found and believed that which has been instituted by him who commanded you to seek only what he instituted.'[4] Christian faith marks the end of all intellectual quest; woe to all the diluters of the simple faith. Though Tertullian, with his superb rhetorical gifts and wide learning, can be said to have gone some way in constructing what he

49

himself denounced as a 'Stoic Christianity', his attack is aimed against any cultural accommodation with the secular world. He delights in underlining the gulf between it and Christian belief: 'The Son of God is crucified: I am not ashamed because it is shameful; the Son of God died: it is credible because it is absurd; the Son of God was buried and rose again: it is certain because it is impossible.'[5]

This is a classic statement of the puritan consciousness of discontinuity. Its massive intransigence is one of the permanent archetypes of possible Christian attitudes to the profane. It belongs, nevertheless, to its historical context. Tertullian was profoundly aware of a need to maintain the Christian identity in the face of insidious threats to it. Not so very long before him, the pagan Celsus had thought 'that it makes very little difference whether we call Zeus the Most High, or Zen, or Adonai, or Sabaoth, or Amoun like the Egyptians, or Papaeus like the Scythians.'[6] The age of Tertullian, the age of Emperor Septimius Severus and his dynasty (193–235), was one of the high points in the spread and reception of oriental and African cults in the Roman Empire. The Emperor Alexander Severus was said to have had a statue of Christ, along with Abraham, Orpheus and Apollonius of Tyana among his household gods. The religious climate of the age was very favourable to the spread and mingling of cults. Tertullian himself commented on the atrophy of Roman conservatism which gave free rein to Serapis and Bacchus 'against the authority of Roman tradition'.[7] Christians needed to face the question: if Christ could be borrowed by Severus, what sort of a divinity was he, really? Christian artists were just beginning to adopt pagan prototypes for the purposes of Christian religious art. Christ, Attis and thrice-greatest Hermes could all be seen symbolized in the figure of the good shepherd. Jesus shared myths and symbols with Orpheus and Apollo, with Hermes and Heracles, Asclepius and Mithras, Helios and others. The figure of Jesus could easily be seen in terms of a saviour-myth common to many religions. Christians who clung to him as a historical person needed some strength to resist the forces which were apt to suck the historical reality into a whirlpool of religious symbols.

Tertullian singled out the crucifixion of Jesus, his death, burial and resurrection in the flesh as the unique historical facts at the core of his faith. These epitomized the 'foolishness to the gentiles'. It would be a mistake, however, to think that the concrete, historical particularity of the man Jesus which Tertullian stressed so powerfully risked being obliterated only by assimilating him to other, competing deities. His person had long been liable to dissolve into mythology in the minds of people who considered themselves to be Christians. Such were a great many of the sects that Irenaeus (c. 130–c. 200), writing towards the end of the second century, considered a serious menace to the Christian Church. Irenaeus enumerated a number of sects with their varied forms of teaching and grouped them together under the heading of 'falsely so-called Gnostics'. He was alluding to the gift of knowledge *(gnosis)* that Christians ever since St Paul regarded as one among the diverse gifts imparted to the Church by the Spirit. Even within the New Testament, however, Paul's disciple Timothy had been warned to avoid 'the godless chatter and contradictions of what is falsely called knowledge, for by professing it some have missed the mark as regards the faith' (1 Tim. 6:20–21). St Paul himself seems to have encountered both what he acknowledged as a Spirit-given *gnosis* enjoyed by some among the faithful as a special gift; and, especially at Corinth and Colossae, something that he regarded as a dangerous and perverse parody of this God-given knowledge. Throughout our period – and indeed down to our own day – *gnosis* retained this ambivalence.

The origins of the movements which have become known as 'Gnosticism' have been much discussed. Plainly, a great many elements went into the making of their distinctive beliefs: among them were the widely current tastes for religious speculation and for magic, eastern mysticism, disappointed apocalyptic hopes among the Jews and Jewish

(Continued on p. 58)

12 The Crucifixion, panel from wooden door of Sta Sabina, Rome, *c.* AD 430. The central fact of the saving history:
It is credible because it is absurd
TERTULLIAN.
see pages 50–51

13 Christ, the tamer of souls, represented as Orpheus, tamer of beasts, detail of sarcophagus from Ostia Antica, 3rd–4th century.
From the irrational, shapeless and formless matter of the Universe the Word has fashioned for himself a harmonious instrument; with perfect wisdom and rational power he brings forth music from its chords
EUSEBIUS, *Laus Constantini*, 11.14.
see page 50

14 Hermes criophoros,
Museo Barracco, Rome.
(like Christ) *obeyed his great father's command*
VIRGIL, *Aeneid*, IV.238.

15 Christ as the Good Shepherd, late 3rd century. Musei Vaticani (Lateran), Rome.
see page 50

12

13

14

16

17

18

16 Gnostic gem, R. W. Hutchinson Collection, University of Liverpool.

Basilides called the almighty God Abraxas; is it not mad raving that each should construct his own God from his imagination?

JEROME, *Comm. in Amos*, II.3.

see pages 58–9

17 *Faith comes by hearing*

ROMANS, 10.15.

pulpit in S. Apollinare Nuovo, Ravenna, 6th century.

see page 65

18 The seat of authority: a bishop's cathedra in the apse of Sta Maria delle Grazie, Grado, 6th century.

Let us be careful not to be insubordinate to the bishop, that we may be obedient to God

IGNATIUS OF ANTIOCH, *Ephes*, 5.

see page 66–7

Christians, following the final disaster of the second Jewish war, and bits of Greek philosophy and Christian doctrine. How much of the resultant amalgam antedated Christianity is uncertain. It does not seem that Gnosticism had emerged as an articulated body of doctrines until well after Christianity had made its own contributions to it. The nature and extent of these contributions varied within extremely wide limits. At one end of the scale, the nature of the gnostic debt to Christianity may be illustrated by comparing two of the books contained in a gnostic library discovered at Nag Hammadi in Egypt in 1946. One of them, a 'Letter to Eugnostos', is a frankly pagan work containing no allusion to Christian beliefs. The other, bearing the title 'Wisdom of Jesus Christ', is a replica of it, but here presented as a secret revelation told by the risen Christ to Mary Magdalene. This is plainly no deviation from Christian orthodoxy; it is a distinct and independent religion receptive enough to absorb some of the trappings of Christianity into its texture.

Some forms of Gnosticism, however, were much more deeply impregnated with Christian ideas. One such work is a 'Gospel of truth' also found in the library of Nag Hammadi. It was probably written around 150 and its association with the Valentinus whom Irenaeus describes as the founder of one of the chief sects is fairly well established. The work contains a powerfully evocative statement of the human condition as an emptiness, ignorance and dereliction, healed by a saving revelation of Christ. The nightmares dissolve with the coming of light, the dreamer, lost, confused and wandering far from himself, awakens and returns to himself. The core of the work is a moving expression of a sense of estrangement in the world and of a homecoming into wholeness. This central core was surrounded in many versions of Gnosticism by an array of symbolism, sometimes bewildering in its complexity. Underlying the symbolism is the gnostic sense of the world of men as a world of darkness, in which the Gnostic feels himself to be a stranger, the member of an élite rightfully belonging to another world. The saving knowledge *(gnosis)* which he receives from the sect reveals to him his origins, the real home where he belongs. According to many versions of the myth the material world is the product of a pre-cosmic fall, as a result of which a fragment of light or spirit has become imprisoned in the world of matter and time. The Gnostic elect identified himself with this trapped fragment and saw in *gnosis* the liberation which would allow him to return. The myth which Irenaeus – rightly or wrongly – associates with Valentinus is an elaborate construction of personified abstractions: Depth, Silence, Wisdom and others rub shoulders with Jesus, the Father, the Church and Paraclete: names which would be familiar to Christians in another world of discourse. The borrowings are transparent; they served to heighten the resonances of the myth, that, even in the potted form in which we have it, has a certain pathos and poignancy. It was, as an ancient account put it, a 'tragic myth' trying to express a vision through symbols: the symbols of deliverance through recollection of origins, of discernment of the fragment of light lying hidden within the darkness of the self, of its liberation. Christian belief has been interwoven into a web of symbols to constitute a world of archetypal images. The Gnostic initiate finds release and restoration to wholeness in confronting the images. In their fables, Tertullian said, the Gnostics seem to 'affirm the common faith in bilingual ambiguities.'[8]

Irenaeus had also been aware that the Gnostics used the same names as Christians used, but as counters in another language. He was the first theologian to ask himself seriously where the difference lay between the Gnostics' 'tragic myth' of redemption and the redemption which he believed Christ to have brought to men. Christ held a central place in more than one gnostic scheme; the question could not be answered merely according to the importance given to him in the teaching of one or other sect. Irenaeus began by rejecting the dualism of gnostic cosmology. In his view the Christian faith did not allow for two worlds, a world of darkness opposed to a world of light, any more than it allowed for two gods, such as many versions of the gnostic myth made responsible for the two worlds. What he opposed to the dualism between darkness and light, with fragments of the light temporarily trapped in the dark but destined to be separated from it and reintegrated in the end, was a single world full of the glory of the one God who created it and to whose providence all its history is subject. The world of matter and time is not alien to man, not to be disowned or rejected as hostile: 'God made temporal things for the sake of man, that by their means he might grow to maturity and bear fruit for immortality.'[9] History, for Irenaeus, was an education by which God led the human race to maturity and would bring all 'to a head in Christ'.

The historical unfolding of God's providence in his dealings with the Jews, then fulfilled in Christ, had already been placed at the centre of Justin's exposition of Christianity. Irenaeus now took up this theme and perceived that what, at bottom, was at stake in the conflict between Gnosticism and Christianity was the obstinate assertion by Christians of a certain series of facts as historical: facts which Gnostics were prepared to dissolve into symbol and to incorporate in a world of supra-historical myth. Christianity may well have been one religion of redemption and deliverance among others; but the redeemer and saviour it preached had been the man Jesus, born under Augustus and executed under Pontius Pilatus in Judaea. To sever the Gospel from its roots in Jewish history – as several Gnostic sects, including the Marcionites, wished to do – was unacceptable for the very reason that to do so would have compromised the unity of God's historical dealings, the unity of the worlds of the Old and of the New Testament, and therewith the historicity of Jesus and of the salvation brought by him. Following the hints he found in Justin, Irenaeus was the first to define sharply the line that divided Christianity from other religions which also claimed the name: the bedrock of Christian belief was faith in a historical person and a history of God's acts. This was the 'hypothesis', the subject matter, he once wrote, about which we may speculate, which we may try to understand in multifarious ways, but which we may not alter.[10] The massive simplicities of the history of God's mighty acts for the salvation of men form the content of his Sunday-school Bible history, the *Demonstration of the Apostolic preaching*: nothing could have been more to the purpose for the 'confirmation of his faith' of his 'beloved Marcianus', to whom Irenaeus addressed the little work, or, for that matter, of his many fellow Christians at the end of the second century.

Irenaeus had not been interested in theological speculation, but he did not reject it provided it was not allowed to dissolve the foundations of Christian faith and substitute something else in the place of God's historical self-revelation in Christ. Clement of Alexandria, a man, as we have seen, profoundly attracted by the philosophical traditions of Greek antiquity, writing not many years after Irenaeus, upheld the ideal of the 'Christian Gnostic' as the type of the perfect Christian. He was as aware as Irenaeus of the menace of Gnosticism. But he maintained the possibility of a Christian *gnosis*: an insight based upon the common faith but elaborated with the aid of special intellectual abilities, perfected in love and kept within the communion of the Church. Indeed he allowed himself to speak of this state as one higher than that of the simple faithful. A conversion to *gnosis* was a kind of second conversion. No two men could be more different than Clement and Tertullian; but the one thing they had in common was what they shared with Irenaeus, the conviction that what defined a Christian as a Christian was, quite simply, assent to a few narrative statements as historical. Their work made explicit and articulate a consciousness that had been present in the earliest Christian community and had subsequently become overlaid and obscured: that what gave Christianity its distinctive identity was not, in the first place, a body of doctrine or a rule of life, still less an ideological alignment in the cosmos or in society, but the proclamation of a few simple facts.

The self-differentiation of Christian orthodoxy from

Gnosticism was a process very characteristic of the Church's evolution. The growth of Christianity brought in its wake crises of self-identification. Each such crisis helped to establish a line between the 'great Church' and the multitude of sects on its periphery, regarded as 'heretical' by the 'great Church', from the viewpoint of its own, 'orthodox', teaching. The orthodox writers of our period (and later) liked to represent their orthodoxy as the original, pure milk of the Gospel, corrupted subsequently by error. Thus Hegesippus, a second-century Christian historian of whose work only fragments have come down to us, is reported to have held that down to the time of Trajan (98–117) 'the Church remained a virgin, pure and uncorrupted . . .'; but later, when all the Apostles and the generations of those who knew them had passed away, 'then godless error began to appear through the deceit of false teachers . . .'.[11] Justin, Irenaeus and Tertullian would all have accepted this model. According to it, heresy is novelty – often thought to derive from the variety of philosophical schools – and orthodoxy the ancient teaching, identical with the teaching of the Apostles. Orthodoxy is original, heresy secondary.

Here and there a Christian thought that heresy was as old as Christianity itself. Origen, for instance, rejected the view of the pagan Celsus that at first Christians were undivided; no important teaching could avoid diversification into sects.[12] But more generally, the model of primitive purity corrupted in the course of development held sway until modern times. It is, however, very difficult to reconcile this with the untidiness of the real evolution of what, with historical hindsight, we are happy to label in neatly circumscribed compartments as 'orthodoxy' and 'heresy'. It is by no means clear that what has subsequently emerged as orthodox was the invariable teaching of the earliest community in every Christian centre. Some early churches look as if they might well have begun their careers endowed with doctrines which elsewhere, or later, would be highly suspect. Moreover, it is becoming increasingly clear from modern studies of the traditions which shaped the New Testament, that the fiction of a primitive orthodoxy does violence to the New Testament itself and to the apostolic community which produced it. As far back as it can be traced, the Christian community appears as one in which divergent and sometimes conflicting traditions co-exist. The emergence of heresy and orthodoxy from a situation much more fluid than Hegesippus would have allowed was also much less unambiguous than he thought. It was a gradual crystallization in the consciousness of Christians over generations, akin to the growth of self-discovery in an individual person. We become aware of our 'selves' as we exclude what we are conscious of as 'not self'. The Church crystallized its consciousness of orthodoxy only in becoming aware of heresy. The relatively undifferentiated consciousness prior to each phase of crystallization contains both orthodoxy and heresy, but not on a wholly equal footing. The options are, at least sometimes, weighted. Though the distinction between heresy and orthodoxy is rarely as clear at the point of decision as it becomes subsequently, it is not always entirely arbitrary. A particular line of development is felt, often in an inchoate way, to cohere better than others with the Gospel, with the bearings of the previous tradition, with the inarticulate preferences implicit in the belief of the worshipping community. In retrospect such doctrinal developments could be seen, as they were instinctively felt at the time, to be homogeneous with the 'mind of the Church' in its previous development. What emerges from the gradual clarification as orthodox rather than heretical is not always the result of extraneous influence, of mere chance or of power politics, as some historians would have it. The prestige of the Roman see and the power of the emperor would in later times often play a decisive part; but it would be too simple to identify orthodoxy with the power to win through.

Hegesippus, Irenaeus and their contemporaries may have been mistaken about the antiquity of orthodoxy and the novelty of heresy. But they did express a sense common to all who thought of themselves as Christians: the sense that the Christian community was extended through time as well as through space. If the community 'here' is in some sense one with the community 'there', the community 'now' is also one with the community 'then'. In its developing self-consciousness the Church always kept alive the capacity to recognize itself in its more mature state as continuous, indeed as identical, with what it had been earlier. The second century is the classic age in which the Christian Church came to articulate its sense of enduring identity. The consciousness of what was permanent, continuous and essential to its nature emerged especially from the 'crisis of identity' which the gnostic movements were for Christianity. In some ways, as we have seen, these sects were very close to orthodox Christianity. Many of them thought of themselves as Christian, and modern scholars have sometimes been ready, even too ready, to accept them as such. They were close enough to mainstream Christianity to make it sometimes difficult to see where orthodox Christianity could be found. Tradition, continuity with the Church of the Apostles, could not, taken by itself, decide the question, for all and sundry were claiming to be 'apostolic'. Many gnostic sects claimed to possess secret revelations entrusted by Christ to one or other of the Apostles or to Mary, and apocryphal writings containing such revelations have come down to us. What was needed was a workable criterion of 'apostolicity'.

One thread in the developing intellectual life of the Church which helped to safeguard its continuous identity was the recognition of a certain limited body of writings as 'scripture'. During the second century a number of works were circulating in the churches and were regarded as suitable for public reading. From the earliest times these included the books of the Old Testament. To them had been gradually added the books which now compose our New Testament, as well as a number of other works. Some of these were gradually extruded, either as 'apocryphal' or as belonging to a later phase of Christian history, suitable for private edification but not for proclaiming the apostolic faith in the Church. The fact that some of the oldest New Testament manuscripts contain some early Christian works not within our scriptural canon may be a residual indication of an earlier and less clear-cut state of affairs. At any rate, by the beginning of the third century a wide consensus had come into being as to a canon of books accepted as authoritative. Some doubts and hesitations remained to be overcome, but by and large the New Testament canon had come into being. By constituting for itself such a canon the Church had made the momentous decision – a decision again crystallized over a long period and latent in some way since very early times – that to this canonized scripture its life and its mind would remain for ever bound. In recognizing a body of writings as containing the word of God, the Church subjected itself to an absolute norm, by which it professed itself to be constituted as the Christian Church.

The books of the New Testament did not, of course, precede the first Christian communities. On the contrary, they crystallized in literary form the traditions current in different communities. In one sense the Church is plainly prior to the Bible; out of its traditions the Bible took its form, and by its traditions the Church decided what was and what was not to count as part of its Bible. Even when the Church had gone a long way towards subjecting itself to the unconditional authority of a canonized scripture, the memory survived in it of an authoritative oral tradition, not wholly merged with the scripture. Increasingly, however, this unwritten tradition was conceived not as containing doctrines, or sayings, which had not found their way into the canon of written books, but as a tradition of interpreting what had come down in writing. This may have contributed to the development of 'rules of faith', statements in which converts confessed their faith which might also serve as yardsticks of what the scriptures could be made to mean. In whatever way an unwritten tradition was conceived, it required a mouthpiece. This need gave rise to the emergence of another thread to safeguard the Church's continuous identity: a permanent and visible organizational framework. A community's claim to be identical with the Church of the Apostles could be tested by a simple two-stage procedure. First, was it united with its own bishop, did it teach what he taught, was it in communion with him? And, second, was the bishop the legitimate successor in a church in which a succession of bishops could be traced without a break back to one or other of the Apostles? If not, was he in communion with bishops of other churches which did have such a link with the apostolic age?

The development of a social structure was the outward counterpart to the process of inner self-definition which took place in the Church during the second century. It was not enough that the Christian community should have a cohesion and that its members should belong to a group with strong internal solidarity. The bonds which linked an individual with his local church, as well as the bonds which linked his church with the Church of the Apostles had to be capable of being made visible. Strong needs seemed to demand that a man's, even more a community's, claim to share the apostolic tradition should be capable of unambiguous verification. The continuously enduring identity of the Christian community was made articulate in the unbroken succession of bishops reaching back to the Apostles.

The bishop came to occupy a central place in the Church, and even more central in the Christian conception of the Church. The origins of the office are obscure; it is more than likely that the development of ecclesiastical office did not take the same course everywhere. Arrangements for leadership must have varied and depended on the chances of local circumstance in the earliest churches. The New Testament contains some hints, but it is on the whole more interested in the community as the abode of the life-giving Spirit than as a social structure equipped with officials endowed with authority and functions. The whole community was the recipient of the Spirit. The function of officials in the Church was to serve the life of the Spirit spread abroad in it. The Spirit had many gifts, and they were scattered broadcast unpredictably through the Church. St Paul, as we know, experienced difficulties with some of its alleged manifestations; he and his apostolic colleagues certainly needed to exercise authoritative supervision over the communities for which they were responsible. The 'freedom of the Spirit' could easily come to look like anarchy and confusion. The true prophet was not always easily distinguished from the false. The early Church soon found simple tests, such as asking for money or wanting to stay more than two days, inadequate to show up the false teacher or prophet. Authority certainly was needed, and equally certainly existed, both in the apostolic communities and later. But always, until other conceptions of ecclesiastical authority came to overlay the primitive notions, the Church was regarded as a ministry. Authority there did not exist in order to rule the community but to serve the prophetic initiatives of the Spirit within it. The institutional framework and the authority vested in office-bearers could only be thought of in a vital dialectical relationship with the manifold gifts of the Spirit entrusted to the whole community.

The new place that the Church came to occupy in society in the Christian Roman Empire from the fourth century, and later still, the place it held in a Germanic, 'barbarian' society, were to change this notion of ecclesiastical office and authority almost beyond recognition, and, with it, to change the relationships between its bearers, the clergy, and the Church at large – the 'laity' as they came to be called. During the second and third centuries this still lay in the future, but already the stress that was being laid on the office of the 'overseer' of the local church, its 'bishop', was beginning to introduce strains into the Church. Early in the second century Ignatius, bishop of Antioch, could write of the bishop almost as the epitome of his whole congregation; and Cyprian, bishop of Carthage (248–58) could go so far as to identify the bishop's with the Apostle's office. By this time a fairly uniform structure of office had come into being. Presbyters and deacons were becoming endued with some of the attributes that had come to raise the bishop above the body of the faithful congregation. Everywhere a growing differentiation within the community is observable, with an ever more sharply defined hierarchy. It has been suggested that this hieratization played an important part in separating the Church from Judaism in this period, when Judaism was evolving in the opposite direction; while in the synagogues the rabbis were replacing the priestly class of Jerusalem, in the Church the 'elders' and 'ministers' were being transformed into a sacred priestly caste.

The Church could look like a rigid hierarchical structure. There were Christians as early as the closing decades of the second century, especially in places such as Phrygia where religious passion and enthusiasm were apt to run strongly, who could see little else than just that in the congregations around them. A hundred years or so earlier an anonymous document of uncertain but early date had insisted on the primacy of the prophetic gift in the Church; if a prophet were a true prophet, the congregation was 'neither to test nor to discern' him.[13] Now the followers of Montanus and the prophetesses of Phrygia with him found the institutional Church quenching the Spirit. Their protest split the Church in Asia Minor, and the movement spread and prospered and was to win the adherence, late in life, of Tertullian himself. The effect, however, of Montanist protest was not to rehabilitate the prophet but to strengthen the conviction in the 'great Church' that the age of the prophets and of revelation had come to an end with the close of the apostolic age.

By the middle of the third century the need felt in the Church to discover and define its own true identity and to maintain and assert it outwardly had been in large measure satisfied. In the course of meeting these needs, however, new uncertainties arose in the Christian consciousness. We noted the cleavage between Clement of Alexandria and Tertullian. Both were seeking to distinguish Christianity from gnostic heresy and both discovered faith in the historical person of

Jesus as the touchstone and bedrock of Christianity. Yet they held deeply opposed views concerning the place of the Christian group in society, on the proper attitude for a Christian to adopt towards the secular world and its culture, indeed, fundamentally, on the nature of the Christian community and the ideal of the Christian life itself. In one view, an irrevocably profane world always opposed Christianity. In the other, Christianity brought fulfilment to a secular world potentially holy. This cleavage between two permanently available options was to haunt the Christianity of the fourth century. It would also affect the development of Eastern and Western Christianity in very different ways.

CHAPTER FOUR

Towards respectability

THE PERSECUTION under Diocletian (284–305) and his colleagues in the imperial office – now reorganized to consist of two senior and two junior emperors – was the last that Christians had to undergo at the hands of the Roman authorities. Known since antiquity as the Great Persecution it was the last attempt to repress the religion which was to claim, within a few years, its first emperor-convert in Constantine I (see Chapter 5). The Church historian Eusebius prefaced his account of the persecution (303–11) with a summary of the state of Christianity on the eve of its outbreak:

How great, how unique were the honour, and liberty too, which before the persecution of my time were granted by all men, Greeks and non-Greeks alike, to the message given through Christ to the world, of true reverence for the God of the Universe! It is beyond me to describe as it deserves. Witness the goodwill so often shown by potentates to our people; they even put into their hands the government of the provinces, releasing them from the agonizing question of sacrificing, in view of the friendliness with which they regarded their teaching. What need I say about those in imperial palaces and about the supreme rulers? Did they not permit the members of their households – consorts, children and servants – to embrace boldly before their eyes the divine message and way of life, hardly minding even if they boasted of the liberty granted to the Faith? . . . And what approbation the rulers in every church unmistakably won from all procurators and governors! How could one describe those mass meetings, the enormous gatherings in every city, and the remarkable congregations in places of worship? No longer satisfied with the old buildings, they raised from the foundations in all the cities churches spacious in plan.[1]

Even allowing for some exaggeration by Eusebius, there is no doubt that, around 300, Christians were to be found in influential positions. Christianity was beginning to penetrate every level of society, into the government as well as the world of learning. The Church enjoyed long periods of peace before the last persecution broke from what must have seemed an almost cloudless sky. The forty years preceding the outbreak of the Great Persecution, especially, marked a great acceleration in the Church's spread in the Empire.

But for the Empire the second half of the third century was a time of severe trial. It came close to political and social disintegration, and economic breakdown. Men were turning to Christianity, whether out of despair of the gods who were failing them so disastrously, or for comfort in the appalling conditions in many places during these years; or perhaps they seized on Christianity to articulate their revulsion from their society. Whatever the reasons, Christianity was making rapid progress and the old gods were losing favour. Serious-minded pagans were alarmed. Porphyry, the disciple of the neo-Platonist philosopher Plotinus, wrote a bitter attack on the Christians around 270. His concern about the extension of Christianity and about the increasing self-confidence, even ostentation, of Christians was not without foundation. Eusebius' testimony to the wide range of liberty enjoyed by Christians and their growing importance in Roman society is borne out by all sorts of evidence. In Nicomedia, an imperial capital, the Christian Church 'stood high, visible from the palace'.[2] A Church Council held in Spain at the end of a bout of persecution in 305 had to deal with problems of Christian clergy and lay people, many of whom were evidently well-to-do and held positions of responsibility in society. Christianity had become, in many places, a flourishing and respectable movement.

Respectability is the key both to its success and to the hostility it aroused among the conservative pagan circles in whose hands the running of the Empire largely rested, who considered themselves the guardians of its well-being, its

(Continued on p. 78)   71

19 Roman art exported to distant provinces: a milestone of the Twentieth Legion, Antonine Wall, 2nd century. Hunterian Museum, Glasgow.

see page 79

20 A local tradition: popular art in Coptic Egypt, limestone block with figure of Apa Pachom, 6th–7th century. British Museum, London.

see pages 79—80

21 The old art and the new: the imperial hunt (*left above*), and the emperor (Hadrian, transformed into Licinius) sacrificing after a hunt (*right above*); (*below*) Constantine addressing the crowds after his victory over Maxentius, AD 312. Details from Arch of Constantine, Rome.

see page 81

22 Jewish art: Ezekiel in the valley of bones, fresco from synagogue, Dura Europos, 3rd century. Damascus Museum.

see page 83

23 Funerary portrait in catacomb of Vigna Massimo, Rome, 4th century.

see page 84

24 The 'impressionistic' style: vault fresco in tomb of Marcus Clodius Hermes (?), Rome, 2nd–3rd century.

see page 83

19

20

21, 22

23,
24

25

26

27

THE FACE AND THE INNER LIFE

25 Portrait head of philosopher, 3rd century.
Liebighaus, Frankfurt.

26 Eusebius, the Christian, gold-glass portrait,
4th century. Musei Vaticani, Rome.

*Why are the most living portraits the most beautiful, even
though others happen to be more symmetric? . . . it is on account
of the presence of soul in them, because they are glowing with the
light of Good reflected in them*
PLOTINUS, *Enneads*, VI 7.22.

see page 84

27 The emperor sacrificing, detail of Arch of Galerius,
Salonika AD 298.

*We wished for the good of the state to correct all things
according to the ancient laws and public discipline of the Romans*
Edict of Galerius, AD 311.

see page 86

culture and its religion. A decisive shift in the balance between them and Christians took place during the third century. The Decian persecution (250) is a landmark in the relations between the Christian Church and Roman society. The force of popular suspicion was not spent, but evidently it had lost enough power to allow Christians to live in security. Almost on the eve of the Decian persecution Origen wrote that they had enjoyed peace 'for a long time now'.[3] But he was also aware that clouds were gathering on the horizon. Political instability was in the air, military disaster threatened; the safety of the state would certainly demand action against the Christians. Origen's fears were proved right. The spread of the faith had mobilized the authorities against it in a new way; now the government itself was initiating persecution. Christians were to be actively sought out and brought to trial. The aim, as always, was to get them to conform with the public cult. In these years of peril it was vital that all subjects of the Empire should rally around the traditions which had secured and upheld its greatness. Much dilution had taken place unchecked during the previous two generations; now the ranks had to be closed. But the persecution was over within a year, and despite another outburst under Valerian, in 257/8, the Church went on to increase and multiply. After the forty years of peace, Diocletian's persecution was, even more than that of Decius, an attempt to rally the conservatism of Roman society against the threat of the religion which was beginning to fill the earth.

Christianity had been an urban religion from the start. It was in the towns of the Greco-Roman world that it spread and it was around the urban centres of the Empire that its structure crystallized. At the Council of Nicaea the order of precedence among the bishops of the great cities seemed an ancient custom. When Christianity was beginning to make some headway in the countryside, the culture of the Christian community was a culture it shared with the cities. Its whole background and development made Christianity as foreign to the underdeveloped, rural world in the Empire as were the ideas and values of the traditional paganism of the urban upper classes. Like Christianity, 'Romanity' was essentially an urban phenomenon. The provinces were Romanized by exporting the way of life and the tastes of the Roman urban bourgeoisie and drawing wider circles into their sphere of influence. Educated Romans might repeat the old commonplaces about Judaism and Christianity being forms of barbarism, and Christians might be content to accept themselves, occasionally, at this valuation. For all that, the distance which separated Christianity from the cultivated paganism of the townsman was very much less than that which separated both from the life and the outlook of the backward peoples of the countryside. This is what brought the Christians into such sharp conflict with the governing classes of the Empire, with the men of letters and the self-conscious, aristocratic guardians of the Roman way of life. They were simply too close to each other for comfort. Instinctively men such as Porphyry, or Hierocles, another thinker who had also written a bitter attack on the Christians and was said to be one of the inspirers of the Great Persecution, saw the followers of Christianity as potential rivals. By the end of the third century they must have seemed to many such men to menace their leading position in society, to be set on a course which would end in a take-over bid.

While the gulf between the educated and half-educated pagans and Christians was closing, there is evidence which suggests that the distance lying between them both and the pagans of the countryside was growing. In many parts of the Empire pre-Roman cultures were being reasserted; or, more precisely, the classicizing Roman crust was cracking and revealing older traditions beneath it. Over much of Europe signs of a Celtic renaissance have been discerned by scholars. 'Arts once scorned returned, nomenclature of persons and places took on a more native sound, the old gods raised their shaggy heads. . . . The Celtic renaissance represented a perceptible and highly significant shift of cultural energy to areas and classes formerly neglected or parasitical, now rising

79

to independence.'⁴ An analogous Berber renaissance has been discerned in North Africa, and there are surer signs of the resurgence of pre-classical cultures in some areas of Asia Minor in which Hellenistic influence had never penetrated very deep. In Egypt, in cities such as Alexandria and Panopolis, Greek was largely the spoken and written language of pagan, Jew and Christian alike; in the countryside Coptic was the language of peasant, monk and heretic. Here, as in Syria, Christianity gave a powerful impetus to the resurgence of a local culture. A literary language and the literature developed in both cases under its influence. But always Christianity served rather to draw these cultures into the main currents of Christian thought than to provide an outlet for local separatism or nationalism. Later, in the fifth and sixth centuries, the Coptic Church in Egypt adopted Monophysite doctrines and rejected the orthodoxy recognized by the government. Coptic Christianity became something not far from a national church. In Syria, opposed theological currents – Monophysite and Nestorian – both assumed Syrian form, both drew deeply on Greek traditions, and both took root and eclipsed the imperial orthodoxy. Attempts have frequently been made to represent these, and other heresies as disguised forms of local nationalism or the expression of local cultures. But it seems more likely that these native Christian cultures had appeared and matured well before the time they came to provide the medium for the expression of autonomous schismatic brands of religion. Christianity appears to have played a centripetal part in their early emergence; it helped to diffuse a common religion, with its ideas, symbols and rituals, and drew local churches into the life of a rich cosmopolitan world. In Africa a dissident Christian tradition was to be kept alive longest among the underprivileged and the poor (see below, pp. 108– 20): but here, too, Christianity acted as a vehicle for the transmission of urban culture. The popular preaching of a learned, city-bred bishop such as Augustine of Hippo (354–430), it has been well observed, 'is part of an attempt to enable a bilingual society to participate in an exclusively Latin religious culture, gravitating around a Latin holy text. . . . Far from fostering native tradition, [Christianity] widened the franchise of the Latin language.'⁵ By a similar process a backward region like Cappadocia could be drawn into the orbit of Greek culture through the work of Greek clergy.

The culture of the towns with which Christianity had identified itself and which it helped to diffuse more widely was undergoing significant changes during the third century. A whole world has changed between the carvings executed soon after 312 for the Arch of Constantine and the carvings of the Hadrianic period re-used on the Arch. The plastic figures of the older work, moving freely in a space in which subtle relations link them to one another, each figure fully individualized, have disappeared and the figures in the new art have become identified with their meaning. The individuality has been pared away and replaced by fixed formulae of expression; spatial relationships have given way to an arrangement designed to emphasize the relative importance of the figures. The stereotype is designed to convey its abstract message; the individual has been swallowed up by his role. Even in official art there was a tendency to abandon the traditional classical art forms and to embrace coarser, simpler and more popular styles. Towards the end of the third century and in the fourth the 'new brutalism' of imperial art seems to reflect a time of upheaval and insecurity; it is the art of men who had lost faith in the classical past. There were attempts to reverse this change; the Emperor Gallienus (253–68), for instance, seems to have sponsored a revival of the styles and forms of the Hadrianic and Antonine age. But the stability of that society, with its nicely blended sense of privilege and public duty, had vanished and with it the measured dignity of its art. The tranquillity of the philosopher now appearing on sarcophagi is perhaps an attempt to recapture something of the tranquillity of that lost world.

The third century also saw the beginnings of Christian art. Christians must have possessed works of art before that time.

They drank out of beakers adorned with figures of Hermes carrying a ram over his shoulders, and they wore seal rings, like everyone else, bearing emblematic designs in common use. In a well-known passage Clement of Alexandria admonished Christians not to use on their jewellery designs such as a sword or a bow, since Christians are men of peace, or a cup, as they are abstemious; let them rather use a dove, a fish, a ship, a lyre or an anchor; these will be reminders of the familiar themes of their faith. Much of the art first patronized by Christians must have consisted of such borrowings from the repertoire of generally current forms and motifs. As their requirements outgrew such modest objects as ornamented cups and rings, when they began to decorate their burial chambers and to lay the bodies of their dead in carved sarcophagi, they were met by a similar process of selective borrowing, over a wider range of pagan (and, probably, also Jewish) art. The artistic vocabulary of the earliest Christian art has been aptly likened to a parasitic language; it forms a language dependent for its livelihood on a larger linguistic system, from a selection of which it was composed. Even the prodigious vitality of Christian art in the fourth and fifth centuries, the development of a biblical narrative art and the vast increase in opportunity, means and scale afforded by fourth-century churches only diversified and enriched what remained late Roman art, patronized by Christians.

Early Christianity was not a favourable soil for the growth of a distinctively Christian art. It shared the Jews' traditional reserve towards the use of religious imagery; its reserve seems to have softened only in the wake of a growing liberalism about the use of representative art in the Jewish milieu. There can be little doubt that Christians adopted Jewish traditions of Bible illustration and that, when they came to build churches, Jewish synagogues provided precedents for some of the interior dispositions, the ornamentation and architectural details. Rabbinic Judaism had relaxed the ancient opposition to religious art and may have provided Christians with the impulse to decorate their places of worship. Our earliest surviving example of Christian painting in a building above ground is the decoration of the baptistry in a house converted into a church at Dura-Europos, a small frontier town on the Euphrates. Executed in the 230s, it is contemporary, or nearly so, with a richly decorated synagogue near by. But Christians were slow to overcome their hesitations about the use of images. To some it still seemed to border on idolatry. In the fourth century, Bishop Eusebius, in the sternest of terms, replied to a request from the sister of the first Christian emperor for a picture of Christ that it would be unheard of. The bishop (see below, p. 98) was no old-fashioned critic of the new Christian establishment, and even when such pictures had become common, there were still churchmen in whose eyes they appeared as not far short of idolatry. It is not without interest that in later controversies, when religious images came under attack, their defenders made use of arguments put forward by pagan thinkers in defence of the value of the symbol. The material image could reflect a transcendent beauty, as every good pagan knew; but it took some Christians a long time to learn this.

Funerary art was not subject to such hesitations; and when church building really began it was under the patronage and the direction of Christian emperors. Whatever the scruples of the bishops may have been, their churches, public monuments of imperial splendour, also acquired suitably lavish interior decoration. In the rise of a Christian art, the role of Christianity may have been receptive, but it was not passive. If Christian art is essentially a selection from the art of late antiquity, it is not an eclectic selection without principle or coherence. Christianity took over instinctively what suited its needs best, and developed those tendencies that were in line with its preferences. One way in which Christian preference showed itself may be seen on the walls of the Roman catacombs. The sketchy, impressionistic treatment of subjects so frequently found there is no more Christian than it is classical or Hellenistic naturalism; both styles, indeed, can be found on the walls of Pompeii. The more naturalistic style, with statuesque figures, solid and self-contained, finished in detail, placed in realistic settings, natural or architectural, so often seen in Hellenistic and Roman painting, is rare in the art of the catacombs. The deliberate sketchiness of a picture intended to suggest more than it contains suited the purpose better. A few lines and patches of colour could evoke a sense of the transcendent more effectively, and certainly with greater economy, than an accomplished classical or Hellenistic work. In the paintings of the catacombs we encounter this concentration on the bare essentials. They often bring into play ideas far beyond the range of the actual representation. At its best this art could be used to create deeply moving and evocative works; it also lent itself for use by an inferior artist to create a picture that would at least be passable. Christian patrons, especially before the fourth century, would often have to be content with the second- or third-rate; their means and tastes would combine to accentuate the shift towards a more popular type of art, less inhibited by the canons of classical taste. They certainly showed no resistance to depicting the greatest of subjects in the simplest of styles.

The artistic developments of the third century were particularly well suited to some of the chief purposes of Christian art. Portrait sculpture, up to the middle of the third century, showed a new sensitivity to the psychic life behind the face. In some of the best portraits of this time there is an intensity which reflects the shifting of men's interests to the inner world. Christians shared that preoccupation; and although portrait sculpture became stiff and stereotyped in the fourth century, something of the same inner intensity came to mark their gold-glass portraits, and the faces in some later mosaics. We have already noted another feature of the artistic change: the disappearance of the form behind the meaning it has to bear, the substitution for spontaneous groupings in space of a mechanical arrangement dictated by role. The increasingly abstract art was singularly suitable for conveying a message, which was precisely what it was most needed for in the Christian Church.

Christianity was not an originating cause, then, of these developments. It took its part in changes that were proceeding on a wider front, and made its own selection from the resources that contemporary culture had to offer.

This was as true of Christian thought and literature as it was of art. The great creative period of Christian thought was in the later fourth century; but already from the end of the second century the Christian school of Alexandria had opened a way for Christians into the Greek philosophical heritage. In the West, with its more rhetorically orientated culture, Christians were also beginning to adopt and to make use of the literary forms and techniques inculcated by the highly conservative educational tradition of the late Empire. Minucius Felix could compose a defence of Christianity in the form of a Ciceronian dialogue, with an urbanity of expression that gives the lie to the charge, placed in the mouth of the pagan Caecilius in the dialogue, that the appeal of Christianity is to 'men innocent of studies, unlearned in letters, to "rude mechanicals".'[6] By the beginning of the fourth century the African rhetorician Arnobius and his pupil Lactantius, whom Renaissance humanists liked to call a 'Christian Cicero', show the extent to which the current rhetorical culture was gaining a foothold in Christian circles. An image was emerging of the civilized Christian, not very different in his tastes and attitudes from his civilized pagan counterpart in the Roman world.

In the first and second centuries Christianity had been suspect and hated as an outlandish minority. By the end of the third century it was still a minority, though much larger and much less outlandish; it was still hated, but hated in a very different way. It was now to the educated townsmen who ran the Empire that Christianity began to make an appeal. Many of them were being won over to Christianity, and it was the others who perceived the danger it was posing to the traditional role of paganism in Roman society. In the Great Persecution at the beginning of the fourth century they tried to rally all the forces of Roman conservatism to eliminate a dangerous rival. Even before the persecution began, the government showed its hand very plainly: 'The Empire has attained its present greatness by the favour of all the gods only because it has protected all its laws with wise religious observance and concern for morality.' So ran a law on marriage, issued in 295. A little later the Manichaean religion was outlawed, for 'it is highly criminal to call in question doctrines once and for all laid down for us and settled by our forefathers'; and fierce repressive measures were enacted against its adherents. Christianity followed shortly after. The real grounds for the persecutions are made plain by the edict issued in 311 by the Emperor Galerius revoking the edicts of persecution: 'We wished previously, always acting for the good of the commonwealth, to correct all things according to the ancient laws and public discipline of the Romans . . .'. Christians were to be brought to their senses and conform to the ancient laws and discipline.[7] The persecution was nothing more nor less than part of a pagan revival. Maximin, Galerius' co-emperor in the East, tried to organize a pagan church modelled upon the Christian, with a hierarchy and a sacred literature; and he circulated blasphemous slanders against Christianity for exhibition in public places and for teaching in schools.

But the persecution came to an end without having accomplished its purpose. 'God who fights on behalf of his Church', wrote the Christian historian Eusebius, 'restrained the tyrant's pride and showed that heaven would fight with us and for us.'[8] With Constantine gaining control, first of the Western provinces and eventually over the whole Empire, Christianity entered upon a new era.

CHAPTER FIVE

The Constantinian revolution

IN A BATTLE near Rome in 312 which Constantine won, as he came to believe, with the aid of the God of the Christians, he conquered his rival and established his authority in the Western provinces of the Empire. 'Throughout the world a bright and glorious day, an unclouded brilliance, illuminated all the churches of Christ with a heavenly light', wrote Eusebius.[1] On the morrow of his victory Constantine granted freedom to Christians to practise their religion and restored to the Church the legal right to hold property. His co-emperor in the East, Licinius, endorsing his policy, joined him in a statement which upheld the principle of religious freedom for all: 'No one whosoever should be denied the liberty to follow either the religion of the Christians or any other cult which of his own free choice he has thought to be best adapted for himself.' Christianity was placed on an equal footing with other religions. Roman public law seemed, for the first time, to embrace a principle wholly foreign to it, the principle of the state's religious neutrality. It was a momentous change, but neither unprepared nor destined to last very long. Constantine's father, Diocletian's co-emperor in Gaul and Britain, had never given the edicts of persecution effect in the provinces under his authority; Galerius in the East, reputedly the prime mover of the persecution, recognized its futility and issued an edict of toleration on his death-bed in 311. The Roman government's toleration of Christians did not originate with Constantine. His was the last of a series of enactments dictated by a growing recognition that the unity of the Roman state could not be built up on its old foundations.

But the notion of a Roman state committed to absolute religious neutrality was too anomalous to last very long. In 324, when he had secured control over the whole Empire by defeating Licinius, now his rival and enemy, Constantine wrote in a very different vein: 'Let those who still delight in error be made welcome to the same peace and tranquillity as those who believe. . . . It is one thing to engage voluntarily on the struggle for immortality, but another thing to constrain others by the fear of punishment.'[2] The neutrality of 312 has given way to what has been aptly described as a 'scornful tolerance'. The emperor has now identified himself with the Christians, just as Galerius had identified himself with the pagans; paganism has become 'error' to be tolerated, just as Christianity had been in 311 to Galerius. The devotees of error are now, as then, expected to come to their senses when their wilful perversity has been overcome by the emperor's magnanimity. If Galerius tolerated Christians in a pagan state in 311, by 324 Constantine may be said to have tolerated pagans in a Christian state.

To speak of a 'Christian state' under Constantine is, however, to anticipate developments of the later fourth century. The legal enforcement of Christianity was the work of his successors. Nevertheless, his favours to the Christian Church amounted to much more than those of a munificent private patron. As early as 313, state subsidies were being paid to churches, desirable exemptions from onerous public duties conceded to clergy, and the emperor is seen taking an interest and intervening in issues dividing the Christian Church. Before long, bishops were given the right to hear legal cases in their courts, Sunday was made an official day of rest, fiscal privileges were granted to the clergy and the authority of the emperor was widely deployed in ecclesiastical disputes, councils, appointments. New churches were being built at imperial expense, and lavish endowments flowed from the imperial treasury. The 'neutrality' of the state hinted at in 312 was very rapidly being eroded.

But the new social relations consequent upon imperial

favour were in the long run far more important than the incipient privileged legal position given to Christianity. From the great crises of the third century much in Roman society emerged profoundly altered. The nature of the imperial office, its relationship to the Roman Senate, the whole structure of government and local administration, all underwent radical change in the dislocation of the social order during the third century and the reforms enacted by Diocletian and Constantine. The reforms brought a new stability; but it was the stability of a largely altered society. The emperors of the later third century who warded off military disaster belonged to a military, rather than to the traditional senatorial, milieu. Diocletian's 'sacred monarchy' completed the process of detaching the imperial office from the framework of the Principate and the Republic. The notion of the emperor as 'the first citizen', always something of a fiction, had become increasingly remote throughout the third century. By the end of the third century no fiction could disguise the fact that the emperors owed their status not to the election by the Senate but to the combined power of their armies and their divine protectors. Whether the emperor was the representative of Jupiter or Hercules, the Unconquered Sun or Christ, he was becoming a semi-divine figure. He towered above his subjects by virtue of the divine power vested in him, and thus he was shown by all the devices of the imperial propaganda. Everything connected with his person and his court was sacred: he lived in a 'sacred palace', issued 'sacred edicts' and when he went hunting he inflicted 'sacred wounds' on his quarry. In the royal hall he sat on a raised dais to receive the 'adoration' of his suppliants; the privileged who were admitted to the throne-room awaited the epiphany of his sacred presence in a religious silence. The curtains before the throne parted, like the clouds revealing the light of the Sun, to reveal the monarch amid clouds of incense, surrounded with torches and greeted by ritual acclamations, beneath the jewelled canopy of his shrine. The office engulfed the human person of its holder. Emperor Constantius II (337–61), who was thought to be something of a playboy by inclination, was transformed by his office: he 'wore the look of a tyrant'.[3] Augustus or Marcus Aurelius would not have recognized themselves in the role of the quasi-divine autocrat whose image Diocletian and his Christian successors presented. The fictions which had disguised the break between the Republic and the Principate had no foothold in this world. They could be kept alive only in a world of romantic fantasy. The ideas current at the court and among the old senatorial aristocracy diverged more and more.

The changing social relationships of the fourth century eased the emergence of a new and, from Constantine onwards, a largely Christian aristocracy of service alongside the old senatorial aristocracy of birth. Constantine's decision to favour Christians was facilitated by the overhaul to which his predecessor had subjected the administration and the court. The Roman Senate now had a very small part to play in government. The vastly expanded bureaucracy in the provincial administration as well as the multiplying posts at the court were being staffed by new men, raised from the lower classes of society. As a result a sharp polarization took place in the course of the fourth century between the old senatorial aristocracy, the Romans of Rome (the 'better part of the human race', as one of them referred to his own class),[4] and the men risen from the ranks of the civil service or the court.

During the third century Rome had ceased to be the Empire's real capital. The centres of government had shifted to the great imperial residences nearer the frontiers: Trier, Milan, Aquileia, Sirmium and Nicomedia. The Romans of Rome were becoming isolated from most functions of government. At court, the new men were in power; and now more and more of them would be Christians. Perhaps the most fateful decision Constantine took was to found a new capital, a 'second Rome', in the East. His city on the Bosporus, dedicated in 330, was to be a new Rome which almost immediately became a Christian Rome. In its Senate the new aristocracy predominated. Here there would never be the polarization between the old senatorial aristocracy and the new men of the court which was so distinctive a feature of Western aristocratic society. Among the Eastern aristocracy, pagan scholars and philosophers rubbed shoulders with a growing number of Christian palace officials, all dominated by a Christian court. Here the emperors did not face a hereditary class with strong traditions of resistance to the new style of the monarchy, with its conservative attachment to old ways and old gods. Under Constantine the countryside, the army and the old aristocracy were very largely pagan. But he saw no reason why the effectively ruling classes should remain pagan; and they did not do so.

Constantine's decision to favour the Christians gave a new twist to the social and political developments of the third century. Through his conversion to Christianity the innovations of the later third century produced a Christian empire. It was no inevitable development but the direction of the emperor's sympathies that opened new doors of power and influence to Christians. Christians of the fourth century were men whom success had taken by surprise. A vision granted by their God to an emperor before a decisive battle had changed the whole course of their history, and gratefully they exploited the miracle which had transformed them from a persecuted minority into a triumphant élite. The reign of Constantine seemed to them to have ushered in a new era. Isolated Christian writers had previously sometimes seen the Roman Empire as embodying a benevolent providence of God. In the unification of the civilized world in the empire of Augustus they had seen a preparation for its unification in the Kingdom of Christ. The 'Roman peace' was a preparation for the ultimate triumph of the peace of Christ. To many fourth-century Christians that triumph was being visibly achieved under the Christian emperors. Eusebius, bishop of Caesarea, friend, publicist and biographer of Constantine and historian of the early Church, saw the first Christian emperor as the fulfilment of the messianic prophecies of the Old Testament. In Constantine God brought to completion

(Continued on p. 98)   91

DENTE·CLEMENTIA·PONT·OPT·MAX·

DOMITIANVS·CAESAR·AVGVSTVS·

28   29

30

31

32

33

34

35

36

37

38

what he had begun in Christ under Augustus; the world was now brought under the yoke of Christ. The emperor who brought about the transformation of the Roman Empire into a 'Christian polity' was depicted in terms both of Hellenistic monarchy and of the messianic expectations of the Old Testament. Constantine was the culmination of God's marvellous saving work. The emperor is the representative of the divine *Logos* upon earth, and his empire is the image of Christ's kingdom. The duality of Church and State are only provisional facets of a single, more fundamental reality, a Christian society.

Eusebius was a propagandist. But his eulogy was more than personal propaganda for his hero. It fell upon fertile ground and rapidly set the tone for Christian conceptions of the imperial office. Expressions like those of Eusebius became common in the course of the fourth century, and rolled from the pens of Christian writers and the tongues of preachers almost instinctively. The emperor was represented as the head of a unitary Christian society, with a divine mission to rule it as the vicar of Christ and to extend the sway of the Gospel among men. Not many churchmen of the fourth century questioned this near-orthodoxy (see below, pp. 105–22). Christendom quickly became accustomed to its new place in society, and almost forgot the streak of apocalyptic opposition to the secular world in its heritage. It was difficult in the new world of the post-Constantinian era to discern the Roman Empire beneath the purple and scarlet robes of the apocalyptic whore seated upon the seven hills, 'drunken with the blood of the saints, and with the blood of the martyrs of Jesus' (Rev. 17:6). Theologians were beginning to speak in terms of a new dispensation: the Old Covenant with the Jews had been superseded by the New at the coming of Christ; so, with the advent of Christian emperors the 'apostolic times', the age of persecutions, were superseded by the 'Christian times'. As foretold and promised in the Scriptures, the persecuted Church had come into its hour of victory. It was now called upon to conquer and to fill the world. Through the agency of rulers, the nations were to be made subject to Christ, the idols broken, the temples destroyed.

It was not until late in the fourth century that emperors began to enact repressive legislation against paganism and heresy. Sporadic suppression of a cult here, spoliation of a temple there, prohibition of secret sacrifices or magical rites were, of course, common. But no systematic attempt to eradicate paganism was made until the last two decades. The emperors had to reckon with powerful pagan forces, whose existence could not be ignored. Constantine, especially, had to be tactful. He could not afford to project a single, unambiguous image to the mixed pagan and Christian public. For many years his coinage, for instance, maintained a careful ambiguity which would allow his pagan subjects to read its symbolism in acceptable, traditional ways. One of the many virtues of the solar monotheism so widespread in the third century was that its symbolism could continue to be used by an emperor who would not wish to be identified exclusively as the earthly representative of Christ, the Sun of Justice. For his pagan subjects he could remain the personification of the Unconquered Sun. In his official acts Constantine could refer in impeccably respectable language – respectable to both educated pagan and Christian ears – to the 'divinity of the great God'; he composed a monotheistic prayer for the use of the pagan majority of his army while the Christians among them attended Sunday mass – a prayer not substantially different from one devised by his pagan rival, Licinius, in 313. But Constantine could still be acclaimed by his soldiers and commended to the gods (in the plural). Even his supervision of the affairs of the Christian Church could be represented as part of the emperor's traditional responsibilities; it was, after all, his task as *pontifex maximus* – a title not given up by Constantine's successors until the time of Gratian (367–83) – to oversee all the cults on whose proper observance the public welfare was thought to depend. In due course, the emperors could relax the ambivalence so carefully maintained by Constantinian propaganda, as the prevailing mood of public opinion shifted. It is impossible to trace at all closely the movement of the balance in favour of Christianity. In 312 Constantine can scarcely have hoped for much in the way of added strength or prestige from his alliance with the Christians. He could not afford to challenge paganism; Julian the Apostate around 360, though prevented here and there by popular resistance from reintroducing paganism, had no need to avoid challenging Christianity. But by the 390s the scales had turned; though Theodosius was faced with a serious pagan reaction, his anti-pagan policies could count on massive support and, indeed, followed in the wake of public opinion (see below, pp. 123–24).

Constantine compensated for all the ambiguity he was careful to maintain before his pagan subjects by the utmost clarity in his dealings with the Church. If we can trust the authenticity of the documents which have come down to us (as we almost certainly can), he thought of himself as God's instrument chosen to accomplish the divine intention to bring all nations to the service of God's holy law, to banish all evil and to secure the prosperity of 'our most blessed faith'.[5] His war against Licinius had become a crusade: 'Under your guidance,' so he prayed to God, 'have I devised and accomplished measures fraught with blessings. Your sacred sign was carried before me as I led your armies to glorious victories. And if the public need should so require, it is under the same symbol of your power I shall do battle against your enemies. I have consecrated my soul to you. . . .'[6] He had been entrusted with a mission and singled out by God to carry it out. In the Empire at large his task was to lead the Christian Church to victory; within the Church, he had to remove error, heal division and ensure the proper preaching and observance of the Christian faith – for God would visit upon the public welfare the condoning of any fault by him. The bishops are his 'dearest brothers', but they were left in little doubt as to who was their master. He was the thirteenth Apostle, to be buried alongside the memorials of the Twelve, and housed in the new church of the Holy Apostles being built next to his new palace in his new capital.

The quasi-messianic image of the Christian emperor found in Eusebius and later ecclesiastical propaganda coincided very closely with the conception of his own office Constantine appears to have held. One of the most continuous threads in fourth-century art is the interchangeability of Christ and emperor in the iconographic repertoire as it was developing. Christ becomes the heavenly emperor, his throne the replica of the emperor's; the nimbus around the emperor's head is appropriated for Christ and his saints; the emperor's arrival at a city and his reception provide the prototype for Christ's entry into Jerusalem. The religious art of Christianity owed much to imperial art. Conversely, the Church found little difficulty in endorsing with its blessing the old images of the quasi-divine emperor. Here and there a traditional trait in imperial iconography might be modified, too blatant a pagan feature removed;[7] but generally the superhuman figure of the emperor emerges enhanced through the blessing of the God of the Christians. His eyes may be raised towards a transcendent majesty which dwarfs his own; but far from being cut down to size, the emperor, a colossus chosen by God, still towers above ordinary mortals. Christians felt no great need to modify the current image of the emperor. In the fourth and fifth centuries the traffic between imperial and Christian iconography tended to be a one-way traffic.

What was true in the sphere of the iconography of Christian art was even more true of Church architecture. It is here that Constantine's patronage of the Christian Church shows itself most tangibly as the revolution which it was in the mode of the Church's existence. From its start, Christianity had had no need of temples, the civic monuments of civic religion. The contrast with paganism must have been in the mind of the writer of The Acts of the Apostles when he made St Paul say 'The God who made the world and everything in it, being Lord of heaven and earth, does not live in shrines made by man' (Acts 17:24). The eyes of his

Athenian listeners would inevitably have turned towards the shrine of their city's divine protectress on the next hill. But Christians had no need for a building to house a God: 'For ye are the temple of the living God' (2 Cor. 6:16), as St Paul liked to remind his congregations. If they needed a building, it was one to house the 'temple', that is, to shelter the congregation of the faithful gathered for their common worship. Any four walls and a roof would do for that; and that is just what Christians did use. They went breaking the bread from house to house (Acts 2:46). In the course of time, as their numbers and their needs for space grew, ordinary houses would no longer suffice and had to be specially converted for community use. Parts of such structures survive, often incorporated in later church buildings. One of the clearest examples of a private house specially converted is the church at Dura-Europos (see above, p. 83) built around 200, converted for the use of the Christian community in 231 and destroyed in 257.

Eusebius tells us (see above, p. 70) that before the Great Persecution purpose-built churches were being put up by Christians, and Porphyry is indignant about the enormous buildings with which Christians were beginning to imitate the temples. Eusebius is thinking of buildings erected for communal worship. These were presumably simple rectangular halls; remnants of walls beneath the church of S. Crisogono in Rome, probably pre-Constantinian in date, suggest that if Christians were in a position to build churches, they would have built something of that kind. Maxentius, who was in control in Rome on the eve of Constantine's victory in 312, may have allowed Christians to build their own buildings while he was indulging his own architectural megalomania. But it was Constantine who gave Christianity a church architecture.

The pagan world had known religious architecture in rich variety. The classical temple was the monumental expression of a civic cult; for the general public, it was the outside that mattered. The interior contained a shrine for a deity, not space for worshippers; the liturgical space was outside the temple, around and in front of it. Whatever else Christian church architecture was to be, it had to provide a liturgical space. Classical religious architecture could provide little that was relevant to Christian requirements. The temple was not intended to contain a liturgical space; the small cult-chambers such as Mithraea and their like, designed for the private cult of a group, met needs analogous to those of the Christians. But by Constantine's time these needs could scarcely have been met by chambers on so small a scale. In any case, the imperial patron would not have been content with such a prototype to give monumental expression to his patronage. That is what church architecture would now have to provide; in this sense church architecture is itself a revolution in the Church's life. A building to accommodate Christian ritual was not sufficient for the purpose; it had to be spacious, splendid, public and imposing. The Christian basilica or assembly-hall, one of the types that emerged as a solution, belonged to a well-established and familiar type of building. Late antiquity knew basilical halls of various shapes and sizes used for all sorts of purposes, secular and religious. Among them the palace-basilica – the imperial audience-hall, where the emperor sat enthroned in an apse as the focus of a cult – seems to be the closest anticipation of the Christian basilicas. But halls of other secular buildings also proved very suitable for conversion into churches, and there is no need to derive the Christian basilica from any one pre-existing building type. It was the natural solution to a problem for which there were all sorts of precedents ready to hand.

The 'normal Christian basilica' came into being only in the course of the fourth and fifth centuries, perhaps in part through the prestige of the cathedral of Rome, one of Constantine's earliest foundations, next door to the imperial palace of the Lateran which he had handed over to the bishop of Rome to serve as his official residence. Constantine's own foundations, however, showed a great variety of form. It is unlikely that all the churches he sponsored were

planned by his own architects;[8] local tastes, liturgical practices, techniques and materials and the say of the local bishop
must all have played their part. Moreover, many of
Constantine's foundations served a dual purpose; they were
designed not only as large congregational churches, but also
as memorial buildings to mark a sacred spot: the cave of the
Nativity in Bethlehem, the spot thought to be the site of the
Crucifixion on Golgotha, or the spot where St Peter's bones
were thought to rest just outside Rome. The churches that
Constantine erected on such sites were elaborate complexes
of several elements, incorporating a basilical-type church for
congregational use, often with a large forecourt or atrium,
combined with a memorial building or shrine over the sacred
spot. For these memorial structures, too, his architects would
be able to draw on a variety of well-established building
types.

Christian architecture, a phrase which would almost have
seemed self-contradictory before the fourth century, shows
most dramatically the impact of Constantine on Christianity.
Large-scale, public church architecture was an index of an
infinitely more revolutionary change in Christianity than
any change that Christianity brought to the evolution of
architecture. Here too, as in the representative arts, Christians
were receptive rather than creative. They were content to
adopt a selection from the forms current in late antiquity and
to develop them for their own needs. In their literary culture
and their thought we find a more complicated relationship
with secular culture. The Constantinian revolution opened
new possibilities and canalized energies in new ways. But the
radical novelty of the situation in which Christianity found
itself was not accepted so smoothly in these spheres. There
was resistance to the new order of things, both within the
Church and outside it. Among both Christians and pagans
there were misgivings about a Church ready to conquer
Roman society and to assimilate its culture. The tensions
generated will occupy us in the next two chapters.

CHAPTER SIX

Protest and establishment

WITHIN the Christian Church the Constantinian settlement created a radically new situation. As we saw in the last chapter, Christians were almost universally ready to accept the emperor's patronage and to exploit the new possibilities of power and influence opened to them by the social changes from which they could now profit. But there were groups of Christians who – though also ready to accept the tangible benefits of imperial bounty – found themselves ill at ease in the new order. The kernel of their attitude was an image of the Church as perpetually opposed to a profane world. 'We rejoice in being hated by the world,' one of them said, summing up their attitude, just as a martyr might have summed it up in the age of the persecutions. This attitude had deep roots in the theological tradition of thinking about the nature of the Church.

The ecclesiology of these 'dissidents' had been forged in the third century, which had been the classic period in Christian history for controversies over penitential discipline. The splits in the African Church in the time of Tertullian, in the Roman Church between Callistus and Hippolytus around 220, and again, in both churches in the 250s, in the time of Novatian in Rome and Cyprian in Carthage, all have a family likeness about them. These divisions heralded rifts which would remain perpetually liable to open, throughout Christian history, for they had to do with some of the most pressing questions of Christian living. What degree of sinfulness was compatible with membership of the Christian community? On what conditions could a sinner be re-admitted to communion with fellow Christians, if he had cut himself off by his conduct? Questions such as these seemed to haunt the Western Church, especially the African and the Roman. We hear much less about controversies over them in the East. The problem of the 'holiness' or 'purity' of the Church is a distinctively Western one; the Eastern Churches somehow took it in their stride. While Western Christians in the third century were debating penitential discipline or the treatment of the 'lapsed' and the baptism of heretics, in the Eastern Church the *cause célèbre* of the century, the 'heresy' of Paul of Samosata, concerned the divine sonship of Jesus.

It is sometimes said that this difference flows from a difference in mentality between East and West: Greeks are credited with a more speculative bent, whereas Latin Romans, with a dormant interest in abstract speculation, are said to have a genius for law, organization and a lively concern about matters of practical action. This may have some truth; but if Western controversies were no more than debates about conduct and about Church order, there would be little purpose in considering them in a book such as this. They were in truth far more than the Western Church's substitute for reflection on serious questions of theology. What was at stake in all these divisions was nothing less than the Church's understanding of itself in relation to the secular world. The Western Church, throughout much of its history, was the arena in which this battle was fought out. The Alexandrian conviction (see above, pp. 47–48) that the tensions between Christianity and secular society, with its values and its culture, could be reconciled provided a model which the Greek Church and, in due course, Byzantine civilization, made profoundly and peculiarly their own. In the East the Christian Church did not think of itself as an élite distinct from the secular world around it. Nor did it feel the secular world as an alien presence, either aggressively hostile to a persecuted élite, or passively inferior, waiting to be moulded by the power of a dominant Christian élite. Byzantine history is fairly poor in dramatic conflicts between the temporal and the spiritual powers; and Eastern thought shows relatively little interest in this theme. Neither in thought nor in fact were temporal and spiritual the poles of a permanent tension. In the East a deeper continuity between them could be taken for granted almost instinctively than was ever possible in the Latin West.

The contrast can be typified most dramatically by juxtaposing the views of Clement of Alexandria (see above, p. 46) with those of Tertullian (see above, pp. 49–51). It would be hard to find better prototypes to point the contrast between a 'theology of continuity' and a radical 'theology of discontinuity'. Their views can stand for the two poles of the tension which is always liable to break out in the Christian mind and which constitutes a permanent possibility of division in the Church. The conditions of being a small and distrusted minority kept the potential division in check in the first two centuries and disguised the latent tensions. Persecution, especially, gave the Christian group the sense of being an élite faced with a hostile world. The actuality of persecution while it lasted, and its imminence, while persecution remained a real possibility, inevitably established a clear line around the faithful community separating it from a visibly hostile world. The Christians were an élite whether they liked it or not. There was no need for any more subtle discernment; the boundary between sacred and profane was obvious. But with the passing of the persecutions the lines became blurred. The brother suspected of weakness, compromise or betrayal in the time of testing constituted the most plainly visible breach of the boundary between sacred and profane; here was one who seemed to belong both to the holy Church of Christ's witnesses and to the world of Christ's enemies. Communities were often torn in such situations by the problem of how to deal with the false brother in their midst. 'It would be sacrilege to have martyrs and traitors together in the Church.'[1] Feelings like this were a transposition of the clearly dividing frontiers of the time of persecution into the new circumstances of its aftermath.

The passing of persecution, however, revealed – in a peculiarly agonizing form – a problem which was permanent and fundamental in Christian existence. St Paul had already admonished the Corinthians not to tolerate the wicked brother in name only (1 Cor. 5 : 11–13) in their midst. Baptism, in his teaching, meant a death to the world and a rebirth in the Spirit. The old man was buried and the new man rose regenerated in Christ. The Church was the 'new creation', the brotherhood of men made new in Christ. But just what moral (and still more, psychological) 'newness' was implied by Christian rebirth would always remain problematic. The existence of 'once-born' men in the community of the regenerated was bound to raise problems. There would always be a tendency for the 'twice-born' to draw a circle within the Church to mark off a 'true Church', outside which lay a false imitation, a 'Church' in name only, perhaps a diabolical parody. For men who felt themselves to be 'twice-born', who had broken with their old lives and their profane environment, the identity of the Church was threatened by the apparent existence of Christians among them who had not demonstrably turned away from their pagan past and from the secular world. 'Christians are made, not born', wrote Tertullian,[2] the archetypal 'twice-born' man. Early in the third century both the Carthaginian and the Roman churches were relaxing their penitential discipline. Men such as Tertullian and, a little later, the Roman priest Hippolytus, saw the change in direction as a betrayal.

It is probably true that until about this time – the first quarter of the third century – the Roman as well as the Carthaginian church had upheld a consistent tradition of rigour. But the existence of tares among the wheat had always been recognized. That there was room in the Church for *hommes moyens sensuels* would generally have been admitted, except among fringe movements committed to the utter repudiation of a pseudo-Church of the carnally minded;

and one chance of repentance would generally have been available even to serious sinners. The true Church was holy, but on almost any showing it had a place for the repentant sinner. In practice, conflicts over penitential discipline naturally looked like disagreements over what must be a question of degree. But radically opposed ways of understanding the place of the Christian group in the world were in fact involved. As we have seen, it was for Tertullian a fully articulated vision, a vision implicit in all his work, of what it meant to be a Christian in the world that lay behind his views on the discipline of the Church and penance. The increasingly stark dichotomy in terms of which he saw the Church and the world ranged against each other in perpetual battle found its final and most intransigent expression in his late works. There he repudiated not only the penitential practice as it was developing both at Rome and in his own North African Church but institutional Christianity as a whole. The true Church, as the Bride of Christ, can have neither spot nor wrinkle; it is the abode of the Holy Spirit and can have no place for the impure and no truck with the works of darkness. The true Church, 'properly and principally' is the Spirit itself; that only, through men of the Spirit, can forgive sins, not the Church which is a 'troop of bishops'.[3]

Tertullian's answer to the perennial problem of unholiness in the holy community brought him to the point of rejecting the institution which tolerated any admixture of unholiness. His theology of the holy, gathered, community of the Spirit abolished rather than solved the problem. But the question continued to haunt the Church: how can an institution which has room for sinners also be holy?

The next phase in the Christian searching of conscience belongs to the years following the persecution under Emperor Decius (249–51). In this persecution many of the Christians of less than heroic mould who must have flocked into the Church during the preceding thirty years fell away, both in Rome and in Africa, the regions we are best informed about. In Rome a local division of the Church, in which the treatment of apostates became one of the issues, ended by giving rise to a widespread movement. The schism of Novatian became almost a worldwide church, which called itself, according to Eusebius,[4] 'the pure'. It was perhaps, never very numerous, but showed a tenacious vitality for centuries.

It was in Africa, however, that the heart-searchings among Christians in the aftermath of the persecution had its most lasting and most revealing results. Here too, as in Rome, there were many apostates wishing to return to communion, and the 'confessors' who had stood firm in the persecution enjoyed great prestige in the churches. Some of them used it to authorize the readmission of the 'lapsed', of people who had been compromised in a moment of weakness. Faced with the prestige of the confessors, Cyprian, the bishop of Carthage, needed to reassert the authority of the bishops; and confronted with the laxity of indiscriminate readmission of the lapsed, Cyprian upheld the firm penitential tradition of the African Church. The situation was the reverse of the Roman case; unlike Novatian, Cyprian was the champion of a (relatively) 'pure' Church identified with the official, episcopal Church. The majority of African bishops rallied to his side, despite the opposition of the Roman bishop; and Cyprian's theology, based on the equation of the institutional Church of the bishops with the gathered Church, pure in the Spirit, became the orthodoxy of the African Church.

Cyprian had read Tertullian, and Tertullian's thought made a deep impression on him. His conception of the Church is both identical with and an inversion of that of Tertullian, who had passionately contrasted the Church of the Spirit with the contaminated pseudo-Church of the bishops. Cyprian rejected the contrast. For him there could be only one Church, and it was the Church of the bishops. Of all ecclesiastical writers Cyprian attached the highest importance to the rôle of the bishop in his church. The New Testament, for Cyprian, spoke of the Church as 'the people united to their bishop and the congregation which remains with its pastor; wherefore', so he wrote to some schismatics, 'you must understand that the bishop is in the Church and the Church in the bishop; and if anyone is not with the bishop, he is not in the Church . . .'.[5] The bishop was the token of Christ's presence in the Church. To leave the bishop was to leave Christ and his Church. But having rejected Tertullian's pure Church of the Spirit as an alternative to the Church of the bishops, Cyprian went on to identify the two.

He transferred what Tertullian had said about the Church of the pure to the Church of the bishops. The gifts of the Spirit were all concentrated in the Church, none were available outside. The sacraments belong only to the Church – outside there can only be counterfeit sacraments. 'No salvation outside the Church' was Cyprian's formula, and it summed up the ancient sense of stark opposition between a holy Church and a profane world. Anyone outside the visible communion of the Church, whatever he may claim, 'is profane, alien: he is outside'.[6] Cyprian's theology is dominated by the doublet 'inside-outside'. 'If the Bride of Christ which is the Church is a garden enclosed' – he liked to use the imagery of the Song of Solomon – 'an enclosure cannot be opened up to strangers and to the profane; if it is a sealed fountain, none may drink there . . . who is outside has no access to the fountain. . . .'[7] 'Truth, light, life and Christ within; lies, darkness, death and Antichrist without.'[8] Such are his antitheses between the true Church of the Spirit and the bishops on the one side, profanity, schism, heresy and unbelief on the other. Buttressed with the Old Testament laws of ritual purity, here is an image of the Church as a tight, closed group, separate and made visible in the world by its ritual purity. Tertullian's consciousness of discontinuity was that of a man reborn of the Spirit; the same consciousness is here concentrated in the group united in sacramental communion with its bishop. That is now the unique milieu of the Spirit and the exclusive home of sanctifying sacraments. In Cyprian's theology the marriage of Church and Spirit was consummated and the dialectic tension between the gifts of the Spirit

(Continued on p. 118)

39 The martyr and the Gospel: St Laurence with Gospel
cupboard, mosaic in mausoleum of Galla Placidia,
Ravenna, 5th century.
*This is the law of the lord my God which I have received from
him*
Acta Eupli.
see page 105

40 The rebirth: font of Church of the Virgin,
Ephesus, 6th century.
*Be submerged, sinners, into the sacred stream for purging: the
water will yield up a new man in place of the old one it has
received*
Inscription from the Lateran Baptistry. ILS 1513.
see page 108

39, 40

ECLESIA EX CIR
CVMCISIONE

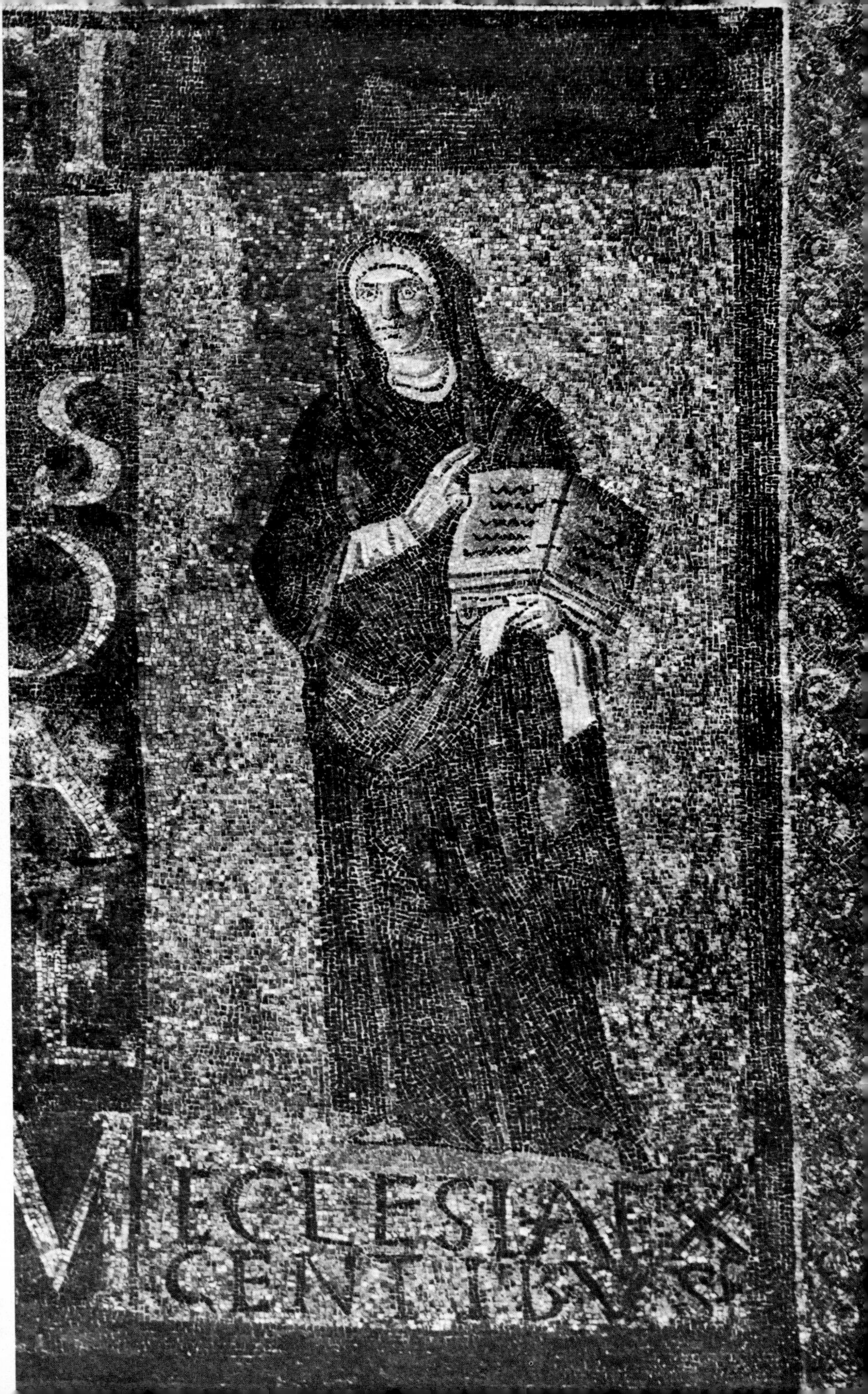
CLESIA EX
GENTIBVS

43

THE BRIDE OF CHRIST

41 Virgin representing Church of the Circumcision

42 Virgin representing Church of the Gentiles,
mosaic in Sta Sabina, Rome, 5th century.

see page 111

43 The separation of the sheep and the goats, mosaic in
S. Apollinare Nuovo, Ravenna, 6th century.

*The difference between the rewards of the just and the penalties
of the wicked, which is obscured in the light of this sun that
shines on us every day, shall be made manifest in the light of the
Sun of Justice . . .*
AUGUSTINE, *De civitate Dei*, XX 27.

see page 122

and the communal institution overcome, though at a price.

Cyprianic theology marked a turning point in Western thought about the Church. The African Church as a whole came to assimilate its characteristic attitude of discontinuity with secular society. After some hesitation in the 250s, the African Church rallied to Cyprian's theology. His death in the Valerianic persecution in 258 set the seal upon his prestige. The next forty years constituted the great age in the spread of Christianity, especially in Africa; the Church which was coming into being here was stamped with this characteristic Cyprianic mentality. It could not find itself comfortably at home in the new conditions brought about by the Constantinian revolution. This conception of what it meant to be a Christian in the world simply did not tally with what it was in fact to be a Christian in the Roman world as it was taking shape in the age of Constantine. The African brand of Christianity, that of Cyprian and Tertullian, was destined to become a religion of protest in the new world of the fourth century.

As it happened, a crisis of confrontation between the two Christian attitudes came very soon. The African Church emerged into the Constantinian era divided. The divisions (which do not concern us here in detail) involved a disputed election to the great see of Carthage. It was as important to an emperor zealous for concord and unity in his Church as for rival claimants to his recognition and patronage to settle the conflict. One of the rival candidates was prepared to fall in line with the baptismal practice which the Roman and the Gallican churches had adopted. He had committed himself, in effect, to accepting the sacramental practice and the ecclesiology on which the Africans had turned their backs in the time of Cyprian. Constantine wanted to settle the schism quickly and asked the bishops of Rome and Gaul to decide who the rightful bishop was. The effective criterion of 'catholicity' (which Constantine was the first to oppose to 'heresy') thus became agreement with the views of Italian and Gaulish bishops. The old Cyprianic tradition of the

African Church was duly condemned by 'the churches across the sea' as the Donatist heresy, and orthodoxy now came to be defined as agreement with the 'catholic' Church.

This 'catholicity' – the Christianity of the 'transmarine churches', as it was seen from Africa – was now pitted against the autonomous tradition of the African Church. Despite the attention given by the emperor to the schism and despite the attempts of his successors to heal it, sometimes by the use of armed repression, Donatism could not be extinguished in Africa. Catholicism, that is churches in communion with the 'churches across the sea', spread most quickly in the urban and heavily romanized areas which were more open to pressure from the establishment. But until the eclipse of Roman rule by the Vandal occupation in 430 and perhaps longer, Donatism survived alongside it, sometimes and in some areas as a powerful rival church. In many towns Donatists had their own cathedrals; in one instance Constantine had to build a new cathedral for the Catholics, their own having been appropriated by the Donatists who could not be evicted. They used the same language, the same worship, believed in the same Jesus and celebrated the same sacraments in their churches as the Catholics. They differed only over what it meant to be a Christian in the world.

A church condemned and disowned by the establishment, deprived of privilege and sometimes subject to forcible repression and legal discrimination appealed to men who had no great stake in Roman society. The Donatists rallied the support, sometimes fanatical and violent, of discontented rural bands, of rebel generals or Moorish chieftains. For all that, the movement was something of far deeper significance to Christianity than a channel for local separatism or for social protest. It provided a model of being the Church in the world alternative to the model of the post-Constantinian imperial Church. It perpetuated in the conditions of the Constantinian revolution an older conception of the function of the religious group in society, which required it to maintain its identity as an élite opposed by the secular world.

The old African ecclesiology, with its own sacramental theology and penitential discipline, enshrined this conception. The tenacious fidelity of one section of the African Church to this tradition brought it into conflict with the European churches and the Christian emperors who took their teaching as the standard of orthodoxy. The Donatist movement thus became the repository both of a regional tradition claiming autonomy in relation to other churches, particularly the church of Rome which was rising to a new pre-eminence, and of a stance of hostility and distrust towards the secular power. The active opposition of the government only sharpened its latent sense that the profane world was in endemic conflict with the sacred. Nothing had changed fundamentally in the Roman Empire when the emperors became Christians – nothing, except the vastly greater number of traitors claiming the name of Christians. The Donatists upheld a streak of 'dissenting' theology in an increasingly Christian establishment, along with the autonomy of a local tradition in an increasingly centralized imperial church. The Vandal conquest of Africa and a century of Byzantine rule, re-established with the imperial reconquest a hundred years later, could not wipe out this tenacious tradition of autonomy *vis-à-vis* both the 'foreign' churches overseas and the government in African Christianity. Until its extinction by the Arab conquest in the seventh century that tradition remained a protest against the 'manufactured churches' of the imperial establishment.

What the African tradition upheld was one of the permanent options of Christian orientation in relation to the secular world. Its stance was shared by more short-lived protests in the Western Church against imperially imposed orthodoxies. Quite large sections of Christianity at one time or other during the fourth century saw themselves faced with a profane world and an apostate church that had succumbed to its temptations. The principal alternative to their way of conceiving the place of the Church in the world was the 'imperial theology' which we have already encountered in Eusebius (see above, pp. 91–101). Eusebius had celebrated the advent of a Christian emperor in the climactic close of his *Ecclesiastical History* with a 'new song unto the Lord'.[9] By the end of the fourth century, most Christians, if they did not belong to a dissenting group such as the Donatists or the Arian Church, were singing the 'new song'. In the West this consciousness of a triumphant Christianity was coloured by a distinctively Western sense of the Church as a spiritual élite. The consciousness which led Donatists to maintain their identity as an élite in a hostile world could find another mode of expression; to a Catholic bishop like Ambrose of Milan (*c.* 339–97) the Church was a creative and purifying élite in a society destined to be absorbed by it, dominated and transformed by Christian influence. He showed that even a Roman emperor could be treated as a 'son of the Church', compelled by the authority of bishops to carry out their will. His younger contemporary, Augustine, bishop of Hippo, expected emperors to 'make their power serve God's majesty by using it to the utmost to spread his worship'. [10] The secular realm was seen by such men as clay to be shaped by the Church. What they shared with the Donatists was the notion of a discontinuous world, in which the sacred existed alongside the profane; where they differed was that instead of defying the world, with the Donatists, they wished to conquer it.

But there was another strand in Augustine's theology. In the very moment when the Church's victory seemed achieved, around 400, when the official enforcement of Christianity by Theodosius (see below, pp. 123–24) had made the whole world a 'choir praising Christ', Augustine turned away from the universal mood of elation. He had shared that elation, and as a Catholic bishop in an African town he was deeply involved in the whole repressive régime of the Theodosian establishment. But, although he upheld the Church's power and influence and even justified its coercive policies, he came to see the 'Christian times' of the Roman Empire as an illusion. Through sustained theological reflection he managed, in the end, to break the spell which the sudden collapse of paganism had cast over so many Christian minds around 400.

As an old man he came to reject the notion of a 'Christian empire' and the possibility of any secular society being transformed and conquered by Christianity. The 'Christian times', the victory of the Gospel won with the aid of rulers whose power had been subdued to the yoke of Christ, now seemed to him the great collective illusion of his age. He had learnt from the distinguished Donatist theologian Tyconius that no human society, whether an empire or a church, was susceptible to so simple an assessment. All societies were inevitably shot through with ambiguity. What both theologians rejected was the notion of the Church as a spiritual élite, whether a persecuted or a dominating élite. Neither of them was content to conceive sacred and profane as two separate spheres, each contained within its own, circumscribed, sociological milieu. In the Church, as in the secular world, sacred and profane were bound to interpenetrate and co-exist until the end. All groups, all institutions were necessarily fraught with this permanent ambivalence. Categories such as sacred and profane could not apply to any actual human groups. It is not altogether surprising that Tyconius had been disowned by the Donatists; nor that Augustine, at least in this respect, was misunderstood, ignored or distorted by the Catholic Church which came to dominate Europe in the Middle Ages. Their critique struck at the roots of Christian group-consciousness, whether in the shape of Cyprianic and Donatist ecclesiology, or of triumphalist Catholicism in Ambrose's or Theodosius' version.

CHAPTER SEVEN

The Christian times and the Roman past

AUGUSTINE introduced a dissonant note into the choir praising the 'Christian times'. It was duly swamped by the prevailing sense among Christians that a new epoch of Roman history was being inaugurated before their eyes. They were conscious of God's triumph in the history of Rome. Despite the uncertainties and conflicts of the generation after Nicaea (325), when the substance of the faith proclaimed in 325 was once more brought into dispute under the Christian sons of the first Christian emperor who had superintended the Council; despite the brief interlude of the reign of Julian the Apostate (360–63) when the privileges conceded to Christians were curtailed and paganism again received official encouragement; and despite the reserved attitude towards the Church's power shown by Julian's immediate successors, Christians were conscious of a steady conquest of the Roman world by the Gospel. The Church's wealth, prestige and power grew, as did its influence in public affairs. Theodosius I (378–95) completed the 'establishment' of Christianity by legislation.

Social pressures towards conformity played a far greater part in sweeping the masses into the Christian Church than repressive legislation was ever to play. Eusebius, already, had been aware of some forces that reinforced the tide of conversions to Christianity; he deplored the 'hypocrisy of those who crept into the Church'[1] with an eye to Constantine's patronage. Around 400, Augustine of Hippo was worried about the influx of half-converted, 'feigned' Christians, as he called them, driven into his congregation by stronger pressures to conform – the pressure of coercion. The last decade of the fourth century saw the flow of edicts outlawing paganism and heresy and seeking to enforce Christian ortho-doxy. But the legislation followed in the wake of more powerful popular forces. In Trier, for example, in the far north of the Empire, pagan shrines that had been in use until the reign of Gratian around 380, were now broken up in a sudden fury of destruction.² From the 380s to the early years of the fifth century we read of idols being uprooted and temples destroyed as far away as Egypt, Syria, Palestine, Africa and other parts of the Empire – often on the initiative of local bishops, backed by the violence of urban mobs or bands of fanatical monks, and generally connived at by the authorities. The emperors from Gratian and Theodosius I onwards were prepared to play the part for which the bishops cast them; they were called to give their own official assist-ance to the work of spreading the Gospel and destroying idolatry. Even Augustine of Hippo was carried away by the tide of Christian intolerance which flowed with unpre-cedented strength in the 390s; and others, like Ambrose, bishop of Milan (374–97), were less inhibited in exerting their influence on emperors such as Gratian and Theodosius. There were clergy like Theophilus, the patriarch of Alexandria, who placed himself at the head of fanatical mobs leading them in violent 'purges' of paganism. Christianity had become conscious of its power to impose itself on Roman society. It had a sense of its mission to conquer the world for the Gospel, and a confidence in its ability to do so very quickly. This sense of mission and confidence could release powerful passions and serve as a channel for the violence never far beneath the surface of late Roman urban life.

Pagans had been watching with anxiety the emergence of aggressive Christian intolerance unchecked, even sanc-tioned, by public authority. Though less clearly than Christians, they too were becoming aware of a new order of things inaugurated by the Constantinian revolution. Indeed it was the pagan Julian, Constantine's nephew, who seems to have been the first to call his uncle a revolutionary: 'the innovator, subverter of ancient laws and traditions received of old'.³ Julian was voicing a disquiet widely felt among the pagan upper and middle classes. Their anxiety, as expressed, for example, in the speech made in defence of the temples by the pagan orator of Antioch, Libanius (in the 380s), was more than foreboding about their own future. They had seen the official toleration of Christians giving way to imperial patronage of the Church; and they saw the growth of a new Christian aristocracy around the court and in the imperial service. But far more insidious, in their eyes, than these swings of the social balance against them was the threat to the values that sustained the Roman state. Rome was a holy city, rooted in its past and the bearer of a destiny for which Virgil had shaped the supreme symbol. The brash new religion was making a bid to replace the hallowed past. The Constantinian revolution had begun as a 'great thaw'; it was now threatening the very foundations of the Empire.

In the last two decades of the fourth century the pagan senatorial families of Rome, such as the Symmachi and their friends, were not merely seeking toleration for their curious blend of antiquarian Roman religion and cults imported from the East; they were seeking to rally men of their class, 'the better part of the human race', to the defence of the traditions on which rested not only Rome's greatness but her very substance and continuous historical identity. This is what was at stake in Symmachus' appeal to the Christian emperors against the removal of the Altar of Victory from the Senate hall in the 380s. What he was pleading for was the Roman tradition itself: the 'ancient institutions', 'the customs of the fathers'. The conservatism of the senatorial aristocracy was brought into play to underpin something much deeper than narrow class-interest: public commitment to a traditional way of life and thought. They knew that in rejecting the claims of the Roman past Emperor Theodosius and Bishop Ambrose were seeking to substitute a new religious foundation for the old, to serve as the basis of a new type of

Christian Empire. The government, under the influence of Christian clergy, centred on a Christian court, and the old pagan aristocracy were now set on a collision course, the former (though trying to conciliate the aristocracy) leading an assault on the past, the latter dedicated to its defence. Thus the 'Christian times' were becoming a watershed in Roman history. The disasters of the early fifth century, especially the taking of Rome by Alaric's Visigoths in 410 (arguably the least serious among them), helped to sharpen the division. Rome's betrayal of her own past in these 'Christian times' could account for all the calamities. In the vocabulary of the pagan opposition, 'Christian times' came to sum up a sense of disintegration and insecurity during these years, and the projection of their resentment on to the new, Christian order.

The last great conflict between paganism and Christianity in the West, at the end of the fourth century, was not primarily a religious conflict. In this respect the pagan opposition to Christianity in Rome differed markedly from the tenacious opposition concentrated, for a long time yet, in Greek intellectual circles, as at Athens. There the philosophical schools kept alive an opposition to the 'reigning doctrine', especially under the virulently intolerant régime of Justinian (527–65); here serious intellectual and religious issues were at stake. In the West the roots of the conflict are entangled with the political and cultural ideals of the senatorial class; the religious tensions were there less acute. Praetextatus, a leading senator of Symmachus' pagan circle, upheld a monotheistic religion in which old Roman and oriental elements blended; Symmachus' more traditional Roman religion interpreted Christianity as one of many alternative routes to the central religious mystery. There was no obvious cause for conflict here. The conflict with Christianity sprang from the combination of two things: the new post-Constantinian mentality which had come to replace the inward-looking faith of the earlier Christians with an aggressive will to power, and the traditional need of the Roman state for a religious foundation. The notion of a neutral, pluralistic state in which all religions were equal before the law was never very congenial to the Roman world. There had been the merest hint of it in Constantine's Edict of Toleration (see above, pp. 87–88), and perhaps Libanius was hankering after it in his oration on behalf of the temples. But the idea never represented more than a fleeting possibility or unrealistic theorizing. For centuries religion had been deeply embedded in Roman public life. The magistrates had always been entrusted with the supervision of the 'peace of the gods', and public life itself depended on divine sanctions. The issue between pagans and Christians was concerned with the religious foundations of the Roman state.

It is important to understand the minds of these pagans if we are to form any realistic estimate of their Christian opponents. We call them 'pagans', but they had little in common with many other pagans. In the countryside, rural cults were deeply rooted, and it took centuries of medieval missions and monastic settlements to christianize many such pockets of paganism. Here and there strong concentrations of paganism survived among the urban masses. Pagan temples continued to be used well into the fifth century, in towns as well as countryside and, on occasion, paganism could assert itself, as it did around 400 when sixty Christians were killed in a riot in a North African township following the destruction of the local cult statue of Hercules. But opposition to Christianity is the only thing these groupings shared with the paganism of the senatorial aristocracy of Rome. Upholding ideas which had changed little since the Republic and Principate, these men still considered themselves as the custodians of the Roman constitution and, therefore, as the rightful judges of the Roman religion. They were not claiming toleration for a private cult[4] but were resisting the powerful thrust of a newly aggressive Christian bid to displace the very foundations of the Roman tradition.

The confrontation generated new tensions within the Christian Church – or more precisely, it revived older divisions of opinion about pagan culture. We have traced some of the currents of thought among Christians in this regard (see above, pp. 42–47). In the Greek-speaking East, and especially within the sphere of Alexandrian influence, there was a long tradition, going back to Clement and Origen, which favoured the study of secular philosophy and literature by Christians. Such a tradition was slower to take root in the Latin West. In some areas, notably in Tertullian's Africa, it was long suspect; sacred and profane were two worlds which had to be kept distinct. Athens was not to pollute Jerusalem. But Tertullian had been writing early in the third century, and even in the Latin West both the situation and the minds of Christians had changed much since. Christianity, as we have seen, had travelled far, even before Constantine, along the road of making its own the culture of Greco-Roman civilization. The new horizons opened to them by Constantine's conversion and patronage accelerated a process already well advanced. The sudden accession of wealth, respectability and steadily growing prestige did not inhibit Christians in their readiness to share the culture of their contemporaries. It may be that we should interpret the vogue of monasticism in the later fourth century as, at least in part, a kind of protest movement within Christianity against its readiness to identify itself so completely with the culture and values of secular society.

But Christians in general were content to assimilate this culture and to become assimilated by this society. They had never, not even at a time when secular studies were suspect to most of them, felt any need to make special provision for their own education. Now that their new social position opened new possibilities to increasing numbers of them, they availed themselves to the full of the educational opportunities provided in the Empire. Before long we hear of pagan professors becoming Christians and of Christians becoming professors. A few cranks objected to sending their children to school with pagan masters. But Christians were generally speaking little inclined to regard secular learning and culture as profane, as can be gauged from the reaction to the decree

published by Julian in 362 which excluded them from teaching in the public high schools. The outcry against this
'tyrannous' measure is enough to show that not many
Christians can have thought the study of secular letters to be
unbecoming a Christian. It was Julian, not themselves, who
thought that the classics and the Gospels could not go together. A few apostatized: men such as Ecebolius, who had
been one of Julian's teachers, and Bishop Pegasius, who had
loved the ancient Homeric sites and taken delight in showing
Julian round them. It is more likely that such men were
opportunists – either in their conversion to Christianity or
their reconversion to paganism, or both – than that they had
become convinced by Julian's propaganda that classicism
and paganism formed an indivisible whole. Others, for
example the Apollinarii, father and son, who turned the
Bible into Greek verse in a variety of metres, composed a
Christian Greek grammar and expounded the Gospels in the
form of Platonic dialogues, were equally exceptional. Most
Christians of Julian's generation appreciated the value of a
classical education and rejected the antithesis which Julian
tried to foist upon them.

Within a year Julian was dead and his decree null. In the
Greek world the wedge he had tried to drive between
Christianity and classical culture left no deep mark. The work
of the Cappadocian fathers showed how little Christianity
had been affected by the episode. But in the West the notion
that somehow Christianity and the classics were opposed
had a longer life. The old charge that Christianity and education did not go together may have had some truth when
Celsus made it in the second century; it had become an
anachronism by the time Julian tried to revive it. But, by a
curious paradox, the anachronism did come to life again in
the generation after Julian.

Julian had opposed 'Hellenism' with the uncultured crudi-
ties of the 'Galileans'. The mainspring of his pagan revival
was the attempt to represent paganism as inextricably linked
to Hellenic culture and thus to deny Christians any share in

the latter, having repudiated the former. Julian's revival was entirely Greek in character; the pagan revival in the West during the following generation was much more Latin in style and spirit. What the two revivals shared, however, was the ideal of a unitary culture sustaining a society based on a common religion. To the defence of this ideal both revivals tried to rally the forces of conservative tradition. Julian's Hellenism had been an amalgam of Greek rhetoric, neo-Platonic philosophy and traditional paganism. The Western revival was less philosophical, more literary: the aristocrats of Symmachus' generation wrote polished verse and letters, imitating the ancient models of excellence. Their whole education inculcated veneration of the great models of the past: they were taught to write like Pliny, Cicero or Virgil. The stress was on form rather than content, and it produced a highly artificial and backward-looking literary culture. They devoted their ample leisure hours on their comfortable country estates to reading, copying and editing the texts of the classics; a good many of our surviving manuscripts of the Latin classics go back to exemplars made at this time. Special care was lavished on the text of Virgil, the poet of Rome's eternal destiny. The *Aeneid* was the pagan Roman's Bible, venerated, copied and expounded as a sacred text. Roman history, too, formed an important part of their interests. Some of them wrote history, others edited the classics of Roman history with devoted care. Their concern for the Roman past sometimes found more public expression: they restored pagan temples, and they lavished their wealth especially on restoration work within the precinct of the Roman Forum, the ancient focus of their loyalties. On beautifully carved ivories they displayed their pagan faith along with their attachment to classical taste. Theirs was no mere learned antiquarianism. It was a devotion to the Roman past in which their aristocratic tastes, their pagan religion and their classical culture fused in a single-minded attachment to a tradition under threat of extinction. The rising Christian tide was threatening to engulf their world; with quiet passion and subdued tenacity these last Romans of Rome were trying to keep alive a whole way of life and feeling, of thought, imagination and public ritual.

Politically their attempt failed when Theodosius crushed the pagan revolt in 394. Culturally, however, it came perilously near to success; the collapse of the pagan reaction could easily have endangered the survival of the classical learning with which it had been identified. In the generation after Julian, and especially around the turn of the century, there is a perceptible hardening of attitude among Western Christians towards classical culture. Classical education had become linked with pagan religion in a new way. The link was forged in the heat of battle. The fiercely self-conscious vindication of their claims to sole rightful possession of classical culture struck a new note, introduced by the pagan reaction under Julian and renewed, intensified, in the 380s and 390s. What Christians had been ready to accept before 360, they were to question anxiously for the next forty or fifty years. The papacy's brief flirtation with classicism under the patronage of Pope Damasus (366–84) was suddenly interrupted, not to be resumed until the 430s (see below, p. 139). Symptoms of an uneasy conscience about the classics abound among Christians at this time. It was the most learned among them, the men who owed most to classical education like Jerome, the brilliant linguist, biblical scholar and translator, or Augustine, who cut short a scintillating career of academic success on his conversion to Christianity, who turned most sharply aside from the literature they had loved. The heavenly judge in Jerome's famous dream, accusing Jerome of being a Ciceronian, not a Christian, was content to accept classical learning at the valuation set upon it by the pagan propagandists: Christianity and the classics belonged to two mutually exclusive worlds. And Augustine, who at school had wept for the death of Dido, as a bishop chided himself for having taken delight in such 'vacuous nonsense'.[5]

The period around 400 was one of the momentous turning points in European civilization, and it could have been

(Continued on p. 138)

44 The Christian emperor (Honorius), with the traditional globe of victory in his left hand, and in his right, a labarum, inscribed 'In Christ's name you shall conquer'. Left panel of Consular diptych of Probus, AD 406, Aosta Cathedral.
see page 123

45 The Patriarch Theophilus standing on a pagan temple *(left)*, and *(right)* monks flinging stones over the Serapaeum, page from *Alexandrian World Chronicle*, 389–92.
And this the Christians call conquest of the gods
EUNAPIUS, *Lives of the Sophists*, 472.
see page 124

46, 47 The pagan revival: ivory diptych of Asclepius and Hygieia, late 4th century. City of Liverpool Museum. They were among Praetextatus' favourite gods in the *Saturnalia*, identified with Sun and Moon.
Sat. I.20.
see page 126

PAGAN SHRINES RESTORED DURING THE REVIVAL AT THE END OF THE 4TH CENTURY

48 Porticus deorum consentium, Forum, Rome, restored by Praetextatus AD 367/8.

49 Temple of Hercules, Ostia, restored by Numerius Projectus AD 393/4.
We ask for the restoration of the cult which has been beneficial to the Roman state for so long
SYMMACHUS, *Relatio* 3.
see page 130

44

45

46, 47

48, 49

50

INTERQVASCVRAMCLYMENI
VOLCANIMARTISQ·DOLOSETI
ADQVECHAODENSOSDIVVM
CARMINEQVOCAPTAEDVMF
DEVOLVVNTITERVMMATERN
LVCTVSARISTAEIVITREISQ·S
OBSTIPVERESEDANTEALIASA
PROSPICIENSSVMMAFLAVV
ETPROCVLOGEMITVNONFRV
CYRENESORORIPSETIBITVA
TRISTISARISTAEVSPENEIGEN
STATLACRIMANSETTECRVDE
HVICPERCVSSANOVAMENT
DVCAGEDVCADNOSFASILLILI
TANGEREAITSIMVLALTAIVB
FLVMINAQVAIVVENISGRES
CVRVATAINMONTISFACIEM
ACCEPITQVESINVVASTOMIS

1   52

EVTYCHIVSMARTYRCRVDELIATVSSATYRANNI
CARNIFICVMQVIASPARITERTVNCMILLENOCENDI
VINCREQVODPOTVITMONSTRAVITGLORIACIRISII
CARCERISINLVVIEMSEQVITVRNOWPOENAPERARTVS
TESTARVMFRAGMENTAPARANNTSOMNVSADIRE
BISSENITRANSIEREDIESALIMENTANEGANTVR
MITTITVRINBARATHRVMSANCVSIAMIOMNIASANGIS
VVLNERAQVEINTVLERATMORTISMETVENDAPOTESTAS
NOCTESOPORIFERATVREANTINSOMNIAMENTEM
OSTENDITLATEBRAINSONTISQMEMBRATENERET
QVERITVRINVENVSQGELITVRIOVTTOMNIAPRESTAT
EXPRESSITDAMASVSMERITVMVENERARESEPVLCRVM

53

54

55

The Symmachorum–Nicomachorum diptych produced for the marriage of two members of the foremost pagan families of Rome, *c.* AD 400.

50 Left panel: Ceres, priestess before altar of Cybele, Cluny Museum, Paris.

51 Right panel: Priestess of Bacchus, Victoria & Albert Museum, London.

see page 130

52 *Vergilius Sangallensis*, MS of Virgil, *c.* AD 400. The pagan's bible, written in a 'majestic lapidary square capital'.
E. A. Lowe.
see page 130

53 Christian classicism: verse epigram by Pope Damasus, incised by the calligrapher Filocalus, *c.* AD 380, S. Sebastiano, Rome.

see page 131

54 Classical civic architecture on the grand scale: Sta Maria Maggiore, Rome, *c.* AD 430.

see pages 139–40

55 Venus portrayed on the lid of the Secundus and Projecta marriage casket prepared for a Christian aristocratic bride, *c.* AD 400. British Museum, London.

see page 140

catastrophic. The impatience of Christians, in a hurry to create a Christian society, opposed by a whole venerable tradition, could easily have entailed a brutal rejection of the whole classical past. Leading Christian intellectuals sometimes came very near to turning their backs on it. Augustine devoted a special treatise to sketching a syllabus for a Christian education to replace the current round of studies. The unifying principle of his educational scheme was the Word of God; its aim was to equip the Christian believer (though, primarily, the clergy) to achieve wisdom. Classical education had sought to make the liberal arts instrumental in the quest of wisdom, 'philosophy'; Christian education would make them subordinate to the one true wisdom to be found in the Holy Scriptures. Augustine's *On Christian Teaching* is a sketch for a biblical culture, alternative to the current culture. Elements of secular learning would, of course, enter into it; for secular learning is needed to understand the Bible – who can make sense of its numerical allegories without some arithmetic, or follow the journeys of Abraham without some geography? But Augustine's formula is ruthlessly exclusive. Secular knowledge is admissible only to the extent that it is useful to a Christian in helping him understand the Bible.

This is no formula for a 'Christian humanism'. Augustine's recipe of 'spoiling the Egyptians' was a recipe for utilizing bits of secular learning where necessary for specifically Christian religious purposes – and as such it would be followed in centuries to come – not an encouragement of interest in the classics or love of learning. Augustine's bridge between Christianity and the classical world was not made for heavy traffic, and could never have served to encourage a wholesale conversion of Christians to the culture of classical antiquity. Jerome and Augustine belonged to the generation of Christian intellectuals which was deeply engaged in the struggle over the pagan Roman past. In that struggle they had almost, implicitly, conceded the claim of men like Symmachus and Nicomachus that pagan past and classical learning formed one indivisible whole. Not without regret, they freed themselves from their own past. Their aim was to liberate Christianity from the spell of the civilization in which it had grown to maturity.

But the christianized society which was rapidly emerging in the Roman world in the course of the fifth century did not, in the event, turn its back on the classical heritage. With the defeat of the pagan reaction in 394 and the suicide of the pagan leader Nicomachus Flavianus, the pagan aristocracy lost a political programme. Except for a brief moment when, a few years later, Alaric's Visigoths were at the gates of the city and during the aftermath of its sacking in 410, the tensions between paganism and Christianity were never again to be so sharply felt as at the close of the fourth century. By a scarcely perceptible process, the sons and grandsons of Ambrose's opponents (see above, p. 125) had become Christians almost to a man. In turning their backs on the old religion, however, they did not also renounce their inherited culture, their tastes, or even, as we shall see, many of their ideas and prejudices. A speedy but unspectacular process won them over to Christianity. By the 430s the old wounds were healing; the deep gulf between pagan and Christian was rapidly becoming a matter of the past. Pagans could now view the age of Symmachus and Praetextatus in a sentimental haze; they would not, in so doing, give offence to their Christian contemporaries. The memory of the pagan leader Nicomachus Flavianus could be officially rehabilitated. The struggle was over, the battle lines were breaking up.

Christians, once more, come into the classical heritage with a clear conscience. The church historian Socrates, recalling the Apollinarii who had turned the Bible into Greek verse in Julian's time, could remark gratefully that 'the works of these men are now of no more importance than had they never been written'.[6] The Christians' stake in classical antiquity could now again be taken for granted. Under the patronage of Pope Sixtus III (432–40) an impressive classical revival in church building in Rome seemed to announce that the Church had taken over the best of the classical tradition. No Roman senator who felt at home in the Ulpian basilica would have felt strange in the new church of Sta Maria Maggiore. This was but one of a homogeneous group of churches built by Sixtus III and his successors in the mid-fifth century. It seems as if the popes wanted to pose before the ancient aristocratic families of Rome, now for the most part won over to Christianity, as the lavish patrons of classical taste. They sponsored an architectural programme which would be seen to rival the churches built in the fourth century under imperial patronage; and not content to rival their splendour, they also revived the vocabulary and styles of high-class official architecture. These, largely bypassed in the fourth-century Roman churches of imperial foundation, could now be adopted for Christian use; their guilt by association was expiated. The new churches gave monumental expression to the growing solidity of the alignment between the papacy and the Roman nobility.

In the course of the fifth century the Roman aristocracy drifted into Christianity. But they did not give up their old pagan interests and habits. They were still carrying on the work of copying and editing classical texts; in their libraries the works of the Latin classics were shelved alongside those of the Christian fathers. Christianity had taken over the pagan classics to such an extent that by about 530, it seems, although there were schools where secular studies could be pursued in Rome, there was no school for advanced Christian studies. In the course of the fifth century Christianity had certainly stepped into the legacy of classical civilization. It also acquired some of the prejudices which that legacy imposed on its devotees.

CHAPTER EIGHT

The triumph of Christianity and barbarism

THE triumph of Christianity at the end of the fourth century removed the inhibitions Christians had felt about making their own the pagan past of Rome. The popes were building splendid, classically-inspired churches and the Christian heirs of the Symmachi and Nicomachi were still editing the texts of pagan – and now also of Christian – authors. In the sixth century, when Italy was under the rule of Ostrogothic kings, a descendant of the Anicii, one of the greatest of the ancient families of Rome, Boethius, embarked on a corpus bringing together in a compact form the sum of Greek philosophy for the benefit of a world to which it was becoming increasingly remote. The work of late Roman aristocrats bequeathed to Western Europe a body of literature which remained the major part of its intellectual capital for centuries.

This conversion of Christianity to the classics was, however, part of a more comprehensive movement of self-identification with the Roman world, with its structure and its culture. The assumption which had gained currency since the time of Constantine that the Roman Empire was the divinely sanctioned socio-political vehicle of Christianity was ubiquitous. For Orosius (see above, pp. 9–10) 'Roman' and 'Christian' were virtually synonymous. 'Christian' had come to define the inner quality of the Roman world; 'Roman' had come to define the outer edges of Christendom. In the fourth century a Catholic bishop could already assume that the Roman and the Christian worlds were coextensive: when Christ, in the prophetic image of the Song of Solomon, calls his Bride from Lebanon, he is referring to the Roman Empire 'where there is a holy priesthood and modesty and virginity: which are not to be found among the barbarians, and even if they were, could not be safe'.[1] The Theodosian era set the seal on the 'Christian times' and gave this cast of mind a firm hold. The euphoria that followed the collapse of the pagan reaction among Christians is most powerfully expressed by the Christian poet Prudentius, writing in the years just after Theodosius. In a long poem he is looking back with calm assurance at the struggle between Ambrose and Symmachus over the Altar of Victory (see above, p. 125); Christianity had emerged victorious. Now, at last, Rome had, 'with entire love, passed to faith in Christ'.[2] But Christ's victory over Rome was also Rome's victory over Christianity; the old 'imperial theme' of the Roman myth is now transposed into a Christian key:

God, wishing to unite peoples of differing speech and kingdoms of varied customs under one ruling power, has determined to bring all that is capable of civilized living under one gentle yoke of concord, so that men's hearts be united by the love of their religion. . . .

To curb their frenzy, God taught all the nations to bow their heads under the same laws and to become Romans. . . .

Come, then, Almighty, enter this world of concord: the whole world receives you now, O Christ, held in bonds of harmony by peace and Rome.[3]

All the horrifying self-assurance of Theodosian Christianity is present in Prudentius' poem. The Empire of Christ was an achieved reality, there for all to see, for the poet to celebrate, and the Church to bless God for. The Roman world had become Christ's; but – though poets and clerics preferred to shut their eyes to the fact – the Roman world was still not the whole world.

The revival of the Empire's fortunes since the later third century had made the barbarian menace on the frontiers seem remote. Only the most far-sighted of Roman writers in the fourth century were conscious of the ever-present pressure on the frontiers. It was a problem for the soldier, not one for the educated civilian to worry about. During the last quarter of the fourth century groups of Goths had been admitted by the government into imperial territory. There were moments of crisis and acute danger, but the Empire had weathered them all. It had even recovered from the disastrous defeat by the Goths at Adrianople (378). To Prudentius and many of his contemporaries it seemed as if the future was assured; the Empire had managed to come through, and now, after all, was not God's power behind it, his purpose bound up with its continued survival? Its collapse was unthinkable. Only a few years before the great barbarian breakthrough on the Rhine (406–07) such disasters seemed remote from the consciousness of contemporary civilians. And when they came to look back upon them, only a few years later, they could not afford to regard them as disasters. 'We ought to praise and extol God's mercy, which has brought the nations, even at the cost of our weakness, to the knowledge of so great a truth' – Orosius is referring to Christianity – 'which might otherwise have remained inaccessible to them.'[4] Orosius had to justify the divine providence which brought the German invaders into the Empire; and he had to combine his justification with the axiom of his faith, that Christianity belonged to and was confined to the Roman orbit. If Christianity could not break out, the barbarians had to break in. It was an axiom widely assumed; it is no wonder that not until the end of the sixth century did any Roman bishop think of sending missionaries to preach the Gospel to barbarians beyond the frontiers. Christianity was the Roman faith, and the Roman Empire the Christian society. Barbarians were outsiders to both, and their only way of entry into the one was by entering both.

But that was less easy than Orosius' shallow optimism suggested. Despite the almost isolated protest against thus linking the destiny of Christianity with that of the Empire by Augustine, most Christian bishops continued to think of the Church within the horizons of the Roman urban society with which they were profoundly identified. The whole traditional development of Christianity, its urban structure and now its classical culture made the notion of a barbarian Christian odd to them. Moreover, many of the bishops belonged to the upper crust of provincial Roman society – especially in areas most affected by the barbarian settlements of the fifth century such as Gaul. In an age when government was collapsing in the west of the Empire, the bishops naturally took over a growing share of the work of keeping life going in their localities. Already given a part in the judicial arrangements of their cities by Constantine, they stepped easily into wider spheres as need dictated. In times of chaos we find them taking the initiative in military matters, organizing local defence, paying troops, repairing town-walls. The diocesan structure of the Church had come to duplicate, almost exactly, the administrative geography of the Empire; the bishop's diocese coincided, generally, with the administrative territory of his city. The bishops were becoming the mainstay of urban society when the resources of central government could no longer play their part in sustaining it. Nothing qualified a man for episcopal office, for example in fifth-century Gaul, as well as wealth and social standing. The majority of bishops in the disturbed Western provinces belonged to the families who were the natural and traditional leaders of this society.

To the discharge of their office they brought the traditional virtues and the practical qualities which distinguished men of their class. But their *savoir-faire* formed part of a style of life which few of them saw good reason to abandon on becoming bishops; and the style of life was profoundly linked with ideals and prejudices to which they were committed by their traditions. The old pride of the aristocrat was now blended with the intolerant Catholicism of the post-Theodosian era. It is important to appreciate the wide extent of common ground between the episcopate, especially in Gaul, and the Christian lay aristocracy. The younger Melania, who refused to communicate with her chaplain because he had mentioned at the prayers of the Mass the name of a lady of doubtful orthodoxy (even though he promised not to do it again) provides one type of example of inflexible aristocratic orthodoxy. We should be wrong not to recognize something of the same narrowness among aristocratic Gaulish bishops. The career and the writings of a man such as Sidonius Apollinaris (c. 431—c. 480) reveal both the strength and the limitations of such a cast of mind.

Sidonius was one of the charmed circle of Gallo-Roman aristocrats, who lived in comfort, though not in ostentatious luxury, in their country houses; they intermarried, visited each other, wrote polite letters and verses to one another, and, often, became fellow bishops of neighbouring cities. The rhythm of their lives was not seriously disturbed by the barbarians whom the Roman government had settled in their midst. A legal fiction disguised the nature of their presence; the foreign invaders were quartered on the Roman provincials as Roman imperial armies. So long as they chose not to blow the fiction sky-high, the arrangement was satisfactory to both parties. The barbarian got his livelihood from the Roman estates, the Roman landowner had enough left to enjoy only slightly reduced opulence after his barbarian 'guest' had had his share. Sidonius himself does not seem to have resented unduly his seven-foot-tall Burgundian 'guests', reeking of garlic, their hair plastered down with rancid butter; he could treat them with an easy, bantering and patronizing superiority. The worst he finds to say about them is that their presence has driven away his muse.[5]

The complaint reveals the kernel of his anxieties about the barbarian settlements. What Sidonius and his friends valued above all things was the literary and rhetorical culture which they regarded as the distinctive property of their class. A friend of his once addressed Sidonius as 'most erudite of men, reviver of ancient eloquence'; erudition, eloquence, antiquity – these were the things which mattered to them. Their education had taught them to admire the classical models of excellence, to pepper their own productions with learned allusions to Greek and Roman antiquity and mythology, and to imitate the styles of Cicero, Pliny or Symmachus. It did not encourage concern for what had to be said but for how it was to be said. It was, as Sidonius himself observed, a 'sterile muse' (though he was thinking of sterility in diction). But artificial and derivative as it is, it would be unjust not to recognize some pathos and dignity in this antiquarian, rhetorical tradition.

Two generations before Sidonius such a culture had been the distinctive possession of a pagan élite, which felt itself charged with upholding it in the face of an increasingly christianized world. It had now become the no less treasured possession of a Christian élite in an increasingly barbarized world. Amid the confusions and uncertainties of the fifth century, accentuated by the legal fictions which obliterated the distinction between Roman soldier and barbarian invader, at a time when political loyalties often constituted a very tangled web, these aristocratic Christian literati took their literary culture as their Ariadne's thread. Where all was in doubt and no ways led clearly to Rome, possession of that heritage marked them out as Romans. The paragon of Roman patriotism, in Sidonius' eyes, was the man who 'amid the storms of war has enabled Latin speech to gain a haven of refuge even though Latin arms have suffered shipwreck'.[6] His correspondence abounds in examples of such praise for men who have kept the flag of Roman eloquence flying amid barbarism. To an isolated governor in far-north Trier he wrote: 'With you and your eloquence surviving even though Roman law has ceased at our borders, the Roman speech does not falter.'[7] This is no mere whistling in the dark. Their speech and their culture gave these men their sense of identity in a world of chaos.

It was, of course, a peculiarly aristocratic identity. Sidonius could be quite as patronizingly superior to the less educated among his own countrymen as to barbarians. 'The educated,' he once wrote, repeating the old rhetorical commonplace used by Libanius a hundred years before[8] and originating with the fountainhead of Hellenistic rhetoric, Isocrates, 'are no less superior to the unlettered than men are to beasts.'[9] The commonplace sums up the snobbery of a man of letters of late antiquity. It is a mirror of the remoteness of his distinctive culture from the conditions of its day. Illiterate town councillors, peasants and barbarians all came under the same scourge. The thought could be given a viciously nationalist or racial twist, for instance when Prudentius wrote that 'Roman and barbarian are as distant one from the other as are four-footed beasts from bipeds, or the dumb from those that speak.'[10] There was a long literary tradition which enabled Ammianus Marcellinus, the distinguished pagan historian at the end of the fourth century, to liken barbarians to beasts who had broken out of their cages and, having tasted blood, become more ferocious.[11] The image could certainly be used to buttress Roman patriotic feeling: for Sidonius, Rome was 'the home of laws, the training school of letters, the assembly-hall of high dignitaries, the head of the universe, the mother-city of liberty, the one community in the world in which only slaves and barbarians are foreigners'.[12] Even Pope Gregory I in the 590s was not above repeating such formulae, but he was no anti-barbarian; and there was nothing peculiarly anti-Germanic about the attitude, nor was it rigidly exclusive. Roman aristocratic society may have been snobbish but it was not often racialist. All barbarism can be cured, all boorishness civilized, as Sidonius once wrote, by the 'wholesome precepts' of classical culture.[13] Germans, provided they become culturally Romans, may aspire to enter the charmed circle. At the court of the Visigothic King Theodoric II, a Gallo-Roman aristocrat like Sidonius, fresh from his country residence, could find himself entirely at home. 'Here,' he wrote, 'you can find Greek elegance, Gallic plenty, Italian briskness, the dignity of state, the attentiveness of a private home, the ordered discipline of royalty.'[14] Of such barbarian leaders Sidonius and his circle were prepared to make use, even to enlist their aid in liberating Rome from enslavement to German barbarians. It was possible for a barbarian to be accepted, provided he was ready to conform to and to accept the values of the dominant classes of Roman provincial society. He could enter, but only on their terms.

The Goths, like the other Germans who settled in the Western provinces of the Empire in the fifth century with the exception of the pagan Franks and English, were Arian Christians. Historians have been very ready to see their Arianism as the great obstacle to their absorption in Roman society. But it may be that we should try rather to understand the Arianism of the barbarians as in large part the creation of Catholic exclusiveness. It is difficult to understand the appeal of Arianism to the Germans except as a defensive reaction to an inhospitable society from which they felt themselves excluded and whose Christianity itself seemed to keep them at arm's length. Attitudes like those of Sidonius, to the extent that they were shared, could only encourage them to turn in upon themselves. The consolidation of un-absorbed and unreconciled Arian barbarian groups within the Roman frontiers, destined to grow into autonomous barbarian kingdoms, is a measure of the failure of Roman urban society and the Catholic Church to absorb them. The fateful alliance of the old aristocratic ideas with the rigid Catholicism of the post-Theodosian age provided the main-spring in the resistance to the barbarian penetration of the provinces; but it also helped to prevent the detribalization of the settlers.

How completely the ideas of Catholic orthodoxy and of being a Roman had become merged in the consciousness of men like Sidonius is best revealed in the moments of crisis. In fifth-century Gaul the crisis came, as it happens, at the very time that Sidonius became bishop of Clermont in the Auvergne. In 466 Theodoric II had been assassinated and replaced on the Visigothic throne by his brother Euric; and Euric was less prepared to comply with the role for which the Goths were cast by the Roman governing classes. It was Sidonius who took the lead in resisting Euric's aggression and organized the defence of Clermont against his yearly attacks.

But it was Euric's attacks on the Catholic Church which seemed to Sidonius to strike at the roots of his Roman identity: 'We fear his designs against our Roman city walls less than his designs against our Christian laws.'[15] The last link with the Roman Empire felt by such Gallo-Roman bishops was the Latin culture and the Catholic religion which gave them their sense of identity among the barbarian settlers. The traditions which had sustained the cultured élite of the Roman aristocracy found a new outlet in the Catholic patriotism confronted with Gothic Arianism.

Not all Christians were as deeply committed to these traditions as Sidonius. A fierce loyalty to Catholic orthodoxy did not prevent Augustine of Hippo, for example, from cultivating a more popular middle-brow culture in his preaching, in order to draw the masses more effectively into Christian orthodoxy. But it would have been unthinkable for a Catholic bishop to take the initiative in trying to absorb the Arian Vandals, who were conquering Roman North Africa in the 430s, into his congregation or into the society around it. The sermons preached by Catholic bishops during the Vandal occupation give us more than a glimpse of the way religious exclusiveness could sharpen existing hostilities. Even when, as here, Catholicism was less aristocratically coloured, it was firmly identified with the social milieu of the Empire. Only very few men could break through the instinctive identification of Roman with Catholic, of Arian with barbarian, and very few could resist the tide which reinforced the divisions created by the invasions with religious barriers. One such person was Severinus, the 'apostle of Noricum' (the Roman province along the Danube, roughly in the area of modern Austria).

The scene of Severinus' activity was a frontier province, made insecure by German tribes which had been subject to the Hunnish empire and released on its break-up at the death of Attila (453). Arian barbarians, Alemanni and Rugi, were on the other side of the Danube. The life of the region was dislocated by chronic insecurity, by interruption of supplies, by the absence of effective government and the running down of organized defence. Like his contemporary Sidonius, Severinus quickly took the lead, in the 460s and 470s, in coping with the daily necessities of life in such disturbed times. The splendid biography we have from the pen of one of his disciples, Eugippius, shows him helping to organize local resistance, supervising the evacuation of civilian populations from towns that could no longer be held, negotiating with barbarian leaders, redeeming captives and organizing an effective, large-scale relief operation based on the network of his own monastic depots and a regular system of taxation which he imposed on the local population. But Severinus did not devote his clear-sighted efficiency and energy only to securing some minimum stability. Immediately on his arrival in the province – he had been a monk in the East and arrived in Noricum as an anonymous, rootless stranger – he had noticed a feckless refusal among the local population to take their situation seriously. His main energies, as hints thrown out by his biographer allow us to guess, seem to have been directed to the often unpopular task of getting people to face the realities. Not being a bishop, his sphere of action was less circumscribed than that of Sidonius; but there were deeper differences of mentality between the two men.

It is idle to speculate about the mind of a man concerning whom the sum total we know comes from a short biography; but from this one thing is very clear – Severinus could never have shared Sidonius' attitude to the barbarians. Everything suggests that they trusted him, some even entered his monasteries, and that his work lay as much among them as among the Roman provincials. What he aimed at was peaceful co-existence of Roman and barbarian; some of the barbarians, notably the Rugi, wanted much the same, and Severinus' work must have played a large part in postponing the breach which eventually came. His biographer, aware that Severinus did not share the anti-Arian and anti-barbarian prejudices which his readers would take for granted, almost makes Severinus apologize for this oddity.[16]

Severinus' career is clear evidence that there were excep-
tions to the rigid intolerance of post-Theodosian Christianity, with its tendency to acquire strongly nationalistic
overtones and to become allied with the conservatism of the
traditional aristocracies. But the cast of mind represented by
Severinus ran against the grain of the prevailing mood. It is
revealing that his disciple, Eugippius, should have found it
necessary to apologize for him. When he was writing his
biography in 510–11, some thirty years after the death of
Severinus, Eugippius was abbot of a monastery in Italy where
Severinus' body had been brought. He moved in circles
which included some of the oldest senatorial families in Rome
and may well have been connected with the opposition to the
Ostrogothic rule which now held sway in Italy. Whether
Eugippius had ever understood his master's mind or not,
thirty fateful years could well have provided good reasons
for some misunderstandings.

In Italy there had been no emperor since the coup (476) by
which a barbarian soldier, Odoacer, deposed Romulus,
Roman usurper of the Western throne. Except for a few
years of war between Odoacer and Theodoric (the Ostrogothic king dispatched from the East by the emperor in
Constantinople), the life of the province had been very little
disrupted. Both Odoacer and Theodoric, when he had finally
ousted Odoacer and taken up residence in Ravenna (493),
knew how to manage those who mattered among their
Italian subjects. The aristocracy were allowed to indulge their
harmless romantic notions and care was taken to avoid more
than the minimum of upset in the assigning of lands to
German settlers. The civil service continued to function in its
accustomed manner, through the well-tried channels, staffed
by its existing personnel. The rulers were nothing if not
meticulously exact in their conduct towards the Church.
They deserved their place as protectors of the Church, now
that the emperor in Constantinople, since 482, counted as a
heretic in the West. Moreover, Theodoric encouraged a far-
reaching programme of building and reconstruction. To a

(Continued on p. 158)   151

56 Medallion of Theodoric, 6th century. Museo Nazionale
delle Terme, Rome.

MAUSOLEUM OF THEODORIC, RAVENNA, 6TH CENTURY

57 A hint of barbarism in the decoration of the rim.

58 In death as in life the Gothic king's tastes were
impeccably Roman.
Love for him among both Goths and Romans grew to be great
PROCOPIUS, *On the Gothic war*, I.1.

see pages 151 and 158

59 The *renovatio* of Roma aeterna by Christ.
Scene of the presentation of Jesus in the Temple
transformed: St Simeon (shown as St Peter) followed
by the priests of Dea Roma (replacing the Apostles)
in front of the templum urbis of Rome (Dea Roma in the
pediment), *c.* AD 430, mosaic in Sta Maria Maggiore, Rome.
see pages 141–3

56

57, 58

59

60

atque egrocanribus pfcpiprcpannrur fiunc ecctecq aquemouard
aur cecuncur; Quciecnomlangueciacaccu dulcius pomr sefecere
columbosfpcnbursoacufic acurpir cibarasfgeaucurmellgruaci tdcm
Nacumuelaquacmffjgidcm lnnomineicadmrpaupcupcipiaccoff
Queaco gsregharcycadiucfhirsegenribursaccar sucucstimcardeg geaquibuf
ludiciofsrucumulupl accaporrormacccde cccipere pondcb&nesleg
que poacsshominiphaebihacrfiuabuer;

FLUUIUS
APE
LE
NA
ESTANUTA
RILIS

SCS MARTINUS

'THE NATIONS SHALL COME TO SERVE YOU,
BRINGING THEIR GIFTS'

60 Barbarians doing homage to the emperor Theodosius I, from the column of Theodosius, Istanbul, *c.* AD 390.

61 The Magi doing homage to Jesus and the Virgin, sarcophagus in S. Vitale, Ravenna, 4th century.

see page 146

62 The first monastic community dedicated to the preservation of learning. The schematic representation of Cassiodorus' monastic foundation of Vivarium, *c.* AD 550. Page from Bamberg MS, 8th century.

see page 160

chronicler in Ravenna his reign seemed like a return of a golden age of prosperity and security.

In every detail the German rulers of Italy conformed to the rôle in society assigned to them by the traditional Roman theory: they were the armed force charged with the protection of Roman civilization. The price exacted by Roman society for its acquiescence in being ruled by barbarian kings was that they should be prepared to conform with its expectations. This meant keeping the Germans on the edge of society; organized as army units, self-contained and ruled by their own leaders, separated from civilian life by their own law and their own Gothic military courts to administer it, they could be tolerated. It was bound to be an unstable partnership, liable to become unbalanced through conflict, both among Romans and among Goths, about the terms of this highly artificial arrangement. The strains began to show when the resumption of direct imperial rule in Italy became a serious possibility, around 520. Among the leaders of the Roman Church and the aristocracy (as so often, in tantalizing proximity) there had always been groups unreconciled to barbarian rule. The dual society in which the barbarian inhabited an enclave separated from the mainstream of Roman life, isolated as an Arian from the Catholic establishment of Roman society, can scarcely have been welcome to the Goths. If they did not relish the rôle of the permanent outsider, there were groups of Romans to whom even this was a violation of their dreams of a re-established Roman order of things with their own emperor to rule them.

The period of Ostrogothic rule in Italy shows the first serious division in the ranks of the Christian establishment about its exclusive commitment to the traditional order of Roman society. Some clergy, especially in Rome, and many aristocratic Christians, descendants of the old families like the Anicii and the Symmachi, found it hard to accept the barbarian in their midst, even in the carefully segregated rôle assigned to him. There were also, however, men like Cassiodorus, with a significantly different attitude, who were prepared to play a crucial part in channelling Gothic rule into the existing moulds of officialdom. These were the men who tried to give some reality to the legal fictions which made the Goths acceptable to their fellow-Romans and helped to avoid any semblance of a catastrophic break with the old order. Cassiodorus was not only one of the top civil servants on whom Theodoric's government depended; he had also written the first history of a German nation to be written by a Roman historian. His (now lost) *History of the Goths* was a work very different from Tacitus' *Germania*. As far as its theme can be reconstructed, it seems to have represented the whole historical career of the Goths in relation to Roman history. Cassiodorus tried to sketch an image of the Gothic destiny as tied up with that of the Roman Empire. The whole historical development pointed towards the partnership of Goth and Roman within the one commonwealth. The creation of a unitary, Romano-Germanic society such as was coming into being in Frankish Gaul could not have entered Cassiodorus' plans; but to the fostering of the more precarious partnership of Goth and Roman in Italy he gave all his energies. It is to the work of men like Cassiodorus, and Bishop Epiphanius of Pavia and their like that we should trace the brief and precarious golden age under Theodoric the Ostrogoth. Genseric, the Vandal conqueror of Africa, had no Cassiodorus or Epiphanius at his side. To that lack we must ascribe the very different shape of the Vandal conquest of Africa from the shape that was to be taken by the Gothic conquest of Italy, perhaps as much as to the difference between Vandal and Goth, between Genseric and Theodoric.

Both kingdoms were annihilated by Justinian's wars of reconquest (533–52). No African Roman regretted the quick collapse of the Vandal kingdom; but in Italy the long drawn-out war provoked more mixed reactions. Cassiodorus retired into monastic life when his work could clearly no longer continue and its achievement lay in ruin; and not all Italians welcomed the imperial troops of reconquest. It would not be long before the liberation they brought to Italy would be described as conquest by the Greeks. In that momentous change the slow weaning of Western Europe from the traditional notions of empire played a large part.

Cassiodorus' retirement to the monastic community he established on his estates in southern Italy around 550 marks a turning point in the history of Christian self-awareness in the Roman world. Only a few years earlier Benedict of Nursia had gathered groups of followers into his monastic communities. Benedict's monks conformed closely to the widely diffused notions current in the orbit of Western monasticism, imported from the East in the main by John Cassian into his community in southern Gaul around 400. Cassiodorus' monastery shared something with Benedict's: it was to be a place of prayer and purification of soul. Detachment from the secular world was an aim it had in common with the whole monastic movement, but in one respect it differed from previous monastic experiments, even Benedict's: this was in the importance that Cassiodorus attached to learning. Benedict had given 'divine reading' a very modest place in the monastic routine; its function was to keep the monk occupied when not busy at prayer or manual labour. Cassiodorus made study, both sacred and secular, the centre of his form of monastic life. How the simpler of his monks took to the programme he laid down for them we can only guess; it is doubtful if his community of learning outlived its founder very long. It did, however, establish something more important: it was the first model of a Christian community devoted to the preservation and the fostering of a culture with which its members were no longer identified.

We must not allow ourselves to be deceived by the resemblance between Cassiodorus' programme in his *Institutes of Divine and Human Learning* and Augustine's *On Christian Teaching* (see above, p. 138). It is certainly close, but only if we forget the century and a half which lie between their composition. Augustine's sketch for a Christian culture was born of a confrontation with pagan claims to sole rights in the heritage of classical culture. Augustine wished to reject that culture in principle, asserting only the Christian's right to borrow from it for his own purposes. For a century and more, Christian men of letters were happily content to disregard Augustine's recipe. By the time Cassiodorus came to apply it, Augustine's hostility to pagan culture had lost its relevance. There was no pagan culture now; Christians had made it their own during the preceding century and a half. Cassiodorus had worked himself free from the stranglehold which that legacy exercised on most Christians during that time; and now, in any case, even the minority culture that classical learning had been, was becoming a thing of the past. It needed to be fostered if it was to be kept in being in a world in which its survival could no longer be taken for granted.

In that lies the difference between the world of Cassiodorus and that of Augustine. It is the difference between the Middle Ages and antiquity, as well as the difference between Latin West and Greek East. In almost every way the end of the sixth century saw a parting of ways.

CHAPTER NINE

The parting ways

THE FIFTH and sixth centuries saw the transformations of
Europe which determined its political and cultural future for
centuries to come. Most of what had been the Western
provinces of the Roman Empire was now a series of barbarian settlements, in the course of development as autonomous kingdoms, and the Roman Empire shrank to what
previously had been its eastern part.

In the last two chapters we have followed the developments which, in the Western Roman world, led, first, to the
appropriation of classical culture by a Christian aristocratic
élite and then, in the course of the break-up of government, to
a growing attenuation of this culture and the preservation of
its rudiments in an increasingly barbarized world, chiefly
through the agency of a monastic élite. We have come to the
threshold of Western Europe's Middle Ages: that paradoxical
phase in which a civilization that has lost contact with its
roots is always seeking to re-establish the broken continuity
(whence the high incidence of 'renaissances' in medieval
Western Europe). If Western Europe lost contact with the
roots of its culture, the East Roman world is above all –
excepting perhaps China – the society which never lost this
contact and never suffered an interruption in its consciousness of its historical continuity. Byzantium had no 'Middle
Ages', it was the East Roman world continued into what we,
from our Western point of view, call our 'Middle Ages'.

From the time of its conquests of the Eastern Mediterranean, Rome had stepped into the Hellenistic legacy. For
some centuries the political destinies of the Hellenistic world

became linked to a world empire centred in Western Europe. The political achievement of the Roman Empire certainly modified the rhythms of historical development in the Hellenistic world. But, as many Westerners appreciated, culturally the Roman conquest could be looked upon as a conquest by Greece of its Roman conquerors. Though Rome had its Greek admirers, there was always a tendency among self-conscious 'Hellenes' to despise Latin culture. For Julian 'civilization' was 'Hellenism'; his admirer, the Antiochene orator Libanius, was not alone in taking a somewhat patronizing attitude to Latin culture. In his great speech in praise of Antioch, Hellenic culture and literature are what raised the city above Rome in grandeur; the period of Roman rule is passed over almost in silence.

Libanius' speech gives expression to an enduring sense of continuity with the Hellenistic past, which was to remain the distinctive note of Byzantine society when Roman civilization was little more than a heap of fragments and memories in Western Europe. There was much to foster this sense of continuity, not least the measure of real continuity in the fabric of society. The little world of the Greek city-states had long ago – since Alexander's day – been superseded by the larger and more impersonal world of an ecumenical empire, and the gods of Olympus who had protected them had been displaced by God, the maker and the lord of all; but no upheaval left lasting scars. Each contributed to reshaping this society and its 'thought-world', as Norman Baynes called it; but through them all runs the thread of an enduring identity. Christianity had played its part in maintaining the thread of continuity and was, at the same time, deeply affected by other, secular, forces with which it was interwoven.

Byzantine and medieval Western society were both Christian. But there are important differences, not only between the two societies but, more particularly, between the ways in which they were Christian; and that is what is of interest to us here. We have already seen (above, chapters 2 and 6) that in the Greek world Christianity was less apt than in the Latin West to be seen as delimiting a sphere of life, of thought or of society, a sphere alternative to and separate from the 'secular'. Western theology lacked the Alexandrian genius for drawing classical thought and pagan learning into a Christian synthesis. It was more apt to contrast Christian and pagan, or sacred and secular, both in the realm of thought and in that of social existence. In the Greek Christian world, too, pagan philosophy was often suspect and – especially in the heat of confrontation – sharply repudiated. Platonism was reputed to go hand in hand with sorcery and theurgy. Greek orthodox theology also had its anti-philosophical strand, not very much less intransigent than could be found in Western Christian thought. But the central tradition of Greek Christianity ran against the grain of such a 'theology of discontinuity'. In the perspective which generally prevailed it was much harder to contrast sacred and secular. We must guard against the danger of pressing all Eastern theology into the mould of Clement of Alexandria's and all Western theology into that of Tertullian's; but they will serve, once more, to point a contrast which is pervasive. The cosmology of Clement and of the Alexandrian tradition, essentially Platonic in inspiration, was hostile to the 'discontinuity' which dominated Tertullian's thought and the African Christian tradition. The latter tended to banish all holiness from the secular world; the Church's sacraments were transactions of grace confined to the closed milieu of the Church or the gathered community of the Spirit – a realm of the sacred, sharply divided from the secular. In the former, the holy was less easy to concentrate into an ecclesiastical enclave, the sacramental life of the Church was necessarily part of a wider universe in which the material world as a whole was more apt to point towards a higher reality as its symbol. The visible world was less self-contained, more firmly built into a single, harmonious universe on many levels of being. An anonymous Christian neo-Platonist around 500 expressed in a classic manner the interdependence of the whole spiritual and material universe in his image of the cosmos as a cascade of light pouring from its transcendent divine source, dissipated gradually in the world of matter, but never wholly extinguished even in the shadows of the lowest realms of being.

Christians necessarily repudiated any divinization of the world, not only the pagan Stoic cosmic religion, but also the widespread cosmic religiosity of late antiquity, though a residual sense of the holiness of the natural world as a whole was never lost in Eastern theology. Reacting to paganism, Christianity left the theme of the restoration of all things in God relatively undeveloped, even in the East; but Eastern theology nevertheless remained inhospitable to the stark way of opposing regenerate with unregenerate nature which dogged Western theology. And it was in the work of an Eastern thinker, Maximus the Confessor (*c.* 580–662) that we can find the most fully developed doctrine of cosmic redemption in antiquity. Through the mediatorship of Christ the whole of man's nature, material and spiritual, is redeemed; and the whole material world and all life is caught up in a dynamic process in which all things are striving towards unity in their source and their goal, which is God. Man is the central link; 'placed above all other things being a kind of very compact workshop', his work and life are the medium through which 'the great mystery of the divine will' is shown forth in nature.[1]

No Western theologian could express such a sense of the holiness of the material world and of ordinary human life. Augustine, rejecting the Manichaean doctrine that the material world is evil and the creation of a power opposed to God, affirmed its intrinsic goodness; but never, in his theology, could the material world be endowed with the religious relevance which it received in the type of spirituality which was instinctive to Greek Christianity.

This always tended to be hostile to any attempt to enclose the holy in a world of its own. This hostility also left its mark on the relationship between the Church and secular society. Here too, the main current of Eastern theology tended to blur the sharply-drawn lines of Western thought. Long after the age of the persecutions Western Christianity was haunted by the image of the Christian group as an élite: if no longer as an élite persecuted by the unrighteous, then as an élite called to provide the lead and inspiration in its world, the moral force to dominate its society, with a right to impose its will on the recalcitrant. The notion of a Church in which the elect kept themselves unsullied by profane society was as anomalous in Greek Christianity as the notion of a Church struggling for supremacy with the lay power. It has been said that there is no Byzantine ecclesiology and no Byzantine political theory; it is certainly true that in so far as both were an outcome of the conflicts from which they crystallized in the West, neither developed in Byzantium.

To understand the part that Christianity played in Byzantine society we need to understand its distinctive theological temperament. But it would be naïve to suppose that the different social orientation of the Byzantine Church, which sometimes seemed so oddly passive to Western Christians, had no other, non-theological roots. A militant Church on the Western model was not only foreign to the cast of mind of Greek Christianity; it lacked the social conditions which made it viable in the West. The survival of a differentiated urban society plainly did much to prevent the emergence of senator-bishops like the Gallic bishops of Sidonius' time (see above, pp. 144–49). Whereas urban life, in the West, came to depend for its continuance more and more upon an urban episcopate, in the East it continued under its own momentum. It could suck bishops, clergy and monks into its turbulent cross-currents. The administration remained present, if not always in full control. The bureaucracy on which continuous government depended and the taxes which paid for it remained ever-present facts of life. There was neither need nor scope for clergy to take over the running of cities or armies. At the end of the sixth century Western bishops could find themselves paying troops and co-ordinating military strategy, for there was no one else to do so; but when, at the same time, a patriarch of Antioch, Gregory, went to restore order among mutinous troops on the Eastern frontier, he did so as a trusted agent of the government. A sensitive Westerner such as Pope Gregory the Great (590–604) was instinctively aware of the differences in rôle and manner that were demanded of him when dealing with Germanic kings on the one hand, and the government or the court of Constantinople on the other.

Compared with the East Roman world, Western Europe as a whole was underdeveloped. The Byzantine world, of course, also had its 'underdeveloped territories'. But the continuing network of urban communities in the East secured the survival of much that became submerged in Western Europe: an elaborate central government, with its provincial and local administration, a system of taxation, a civil service with its traditions of learning and professionalism (a 'Byzantine Confucianism', as it has been aptly called), a lively commercial life and a money economy. Bishops, clergy and monks had to fit into a society infinitely more differentiated than that which was taking shape over most of the Western world. The crisis of the third century had made the whole Roman world more military in character. Public office in the time of Constantine came to be thought of as military service and was organized on the analogy of army units. The emperors themselves, beneath their divine aura, were military figures. Even for his retirement Diocletian had chosen a palace built on the model of a Roman fort. The collapse of government and the barbarian invasions accentuated this trend in the West; civilian society was on the wane. Life came to depend more and more on the soldier and the bishop. In the Byzantine world, by contrast, the civilian came into his own again, and this civilian character remained firmly ingrained in Byzantine life until its end. 'Even the tenth-century Byzantine general with the sweet-scented pastilles for his tent and his travelling library on the art of war was rather a civilian character by comparison with the standards of the contemporary West.'[2]

167

This was too complex a society for the Church to dominate. In barbarian Europe the Church became the hub around which town life turned. Its rôle was decisive in the development of towns until reviving trade, later in the Middle Ages, came to accelerate and to modify the rhythms of urban life. In the sub-Roman centuries the survival of towns generally depended on their being also the seats of bishoprics, or holy places. Often the centre of gravity of ancient cities shifted away from the old civic centres towards the cathedral or cult centre on the edges of the city or in a suburb. In the East Roman world the Church invaded the market-place early and took its place more readily among the centres of public life, alongside the imperial palaces, the forum, the baths and the hippodrome. If Western society in the Middle Ages can be described as dcminated by the Church, Byzantine society is perhaps better described as permeated by Christanity. The polarization of Christian and pagan, of sacred and secular, which took root in the West, had never been possible in the East. In the 350s the pagan philosopher Themistius had moved with greater ease in the court of Christian emperors than among the supporters of the pagan Julian. Such symbiosis required a social space, and Constantinople and the other great Hellenistic cities provided it. Here men could find the physical conditions and the social opportunities for varied encounters and relationships. The life of the city was, of its nature, hostile to any drastic simplification of rôles; it maintained among its citizens a permanent consciousness of overlapping groups and interpenetrating rôles. It could take the tactful pagan and the tactless saint equally in its stride. The quality which had made Constantinople – 'the Christ-loving city'[3] – hospitable to the pagan Themistius in the fourth century also made it hospitable, at the end of the fifth century, to Daniel the Stylite. En route for the Holy Land, prior to retiring upon a pillar in the desert, he was turned back through a vision of a holy man to a 'second Jerusalem, Constantinople by name', where he established himself on a pillar and became valued as something of a talisman, a source of diplomatic advice, an arbiter of orthodoxy and occasionally a gadfly. The peculiar relationship of a saint like Daniel to the lay world of the capital is a measure of its capacity to absorb and to make use of the outsider. Byzantine society knew the value of variety and tension, and – though sometimes the tensions snapped and flared into conflict – generally knew how to profit from them.

The apparent paradoxes of Byzantine literary and philosophical culture are linked both with this multiformity of Byzantine society and with the absence of a clear line of demarcation between sacred and secular in the Greek Christian tradition. Christianity had come to clothe the outward forms of all public life; its ritual consecrated public functions and enriched their meaning with far-reaching symbolism. Christianity reached every corner of Byzantine life; to be a 'Roman' (meaning, of course, a Byzantine) meant to be a member of the Orthodox Greek Church. Nevertheless, the Byzantine world found both the interest and the energy to keep alive an older pagan culture and literature in a way which did not long remain possible in the Christian West, and had never been possible on the same scale. A more than casual acquaintance with Homer could be reckoned on among courtiers; Plato and Aristotle were among the authors studied by aspirants to the civil service; and we do not find among Greek Christians the need to justify the value of the pagan classics and of secular learning which seems to be a recurrent compulsion among Western writers. Byzantine scholars and men of letters felt no conscious conflict in being heirs of the classical past and also being Christians. Their Christianity was receptive enough to exist alongside their secular culture, without needing to justify or seeking to dominate it. They could allow themselves to indulge a cultivated, deliberate Hellenism, which totally eclipsed their Christianity, without the slightest sense of tension or compromise. The craftsmen of the capital adorned the Great Palace of the Christian emperors with superb mosaics continuing the pagan traditions unchanged; the repertoire of Greek mythology long continued to furnish subjects to Byzantine miniature painters and ivory carvers. Byzantine historians such as Procopius and Agathias in the sixth century could give their work a deceptively pagan appearance through the affectation which made them avoid openly Christian language. Their classicism produced a 'secular' history in the pagan tradition beneath which their own Christian beliefs can nevertheless be discerned. Just as the pagan historian Ammianus had wanted to write like Tacitus, Procopius wanted to write like Thucydides; but the Latin West never produced a Christian Ammianus. Norman Baynes, as so often, went to the heart of the matter when he wrote that 'the conscious archaism of East Roman writers, their arduous efforts to preserve the literary style of the classical age – these are not merely the concern of the philologist, they are part of the history of Byzantine thought. Whenever the Empire was strongest it tended to reassert its close and continuous connexion with the Hellenic past. . . .'[5] The sense of continuity with the classic age of Greece was as strong as the continuity of the Greek Christian tradition, embodied, for the common man, above all in the liturgy. The double identity produced in Byzantine culture a unique blend of veneration for a static idealized past, and a dynamism which the sway of a continuous tradition never extinguished. On every level, from the art of popular devotion in remote monasteries to the officially sponsored art of the capital, the interplay of the two currents proved inexhaustibly productive.

For all its vitality this culture was a precarious achievement, the menace of the barbarian never very remote. The danger served, if anything, to heighten Byzantine self-confidence. The stability of the Empire was rooted in God's will: His protection was the guarantee of its survival in the direst peril. The patron saint was at least as important as the town walls. Byzantine society was committed to the double mission of preserving civilization amid barbarism and

Christianity amid idolatry. The tenacious conservatism of a whole culture was harnessed to the energetic defence of what Baynes called a 'way of life'. It is easy to understand the pride which in the eyes of a visitor from Western barbarian Europe was sheer arrogant insularity. When the Italian bishop Liutprand visited Constantinople in the tenth century, he entered a world very different from that which his own had become. His first reaction was a naïve, uninhibited admiration for its sophistication and splendour. But the strangeness could easily engender suspicion. On his second visit, twenty years later, angry recrimination displaced his admiration. By Western standards Liutprand was an educated and intelligent man; but what lay entirely beyond his comprehension was the force of a whole thought-world in which the notion of a 'Roman Empire' in barbarian hands – Liutprand was the ambassador of a German king who claimed the title of Roman emperor – just could not make sense.

In the later sixth century East and West were already beginning to close in on themselves, although the government still thought of the Western provinces as part of the Empire. The Emperor Maurice (582–602) seems indeed still to have envisaged the re-establishment of imperial authority over them once more. Renewed barbarian conquests had made Justinian's reconquest short-lived. Much of Italy was now in the power of the Lombards; the Goths were building a strong state in Spain while the Franks were consolidating their power in Gaul and the English in Britain. Slav peoples were settling in the Balkan peninsula, the traditional bridge between Greek East and Latin West. In Africa the imperial authorities inherited the permanent difficulties of enforcing the authority of a central government, be it that of Roman or Vandal, on the indigenous Moorish peoples. Beneath the fictions which enabled administrators, scholars and modern historians to deceive themselves into thinking that the old order had not passed away, a new world was in fact coming into being. Like many of the greatest changes, it is not easy to pin-point; but one can feel the gulf that divided the world of

(Continued on p. 178)   171

63

64

65

66

67

68

70 71   72

73

74

Emperor Maurice and Pope Gregory the Great at the end of the sixth century from the world of Emperor Anastasius and King Theodoric the Ostrogoth less than a hundred years before.

The extent to which Latin Western Europe and the Byzantine world had in fact come to move in their relatively isolated orbits is as plainly visible in the imagination of contemporaries as in the political fragmentation. Compare the horizons of two educated men writing at this time: Gregory, bishop of Tours, the author of a *History of the Franks*, and Evagrius, a lay official in the circle of the patriarch of Antioch, the author of a *History of the Church* from 431. Both authors ended their work with contemporary history, brought down to the 590s. Gregory of Tours was dimly aware of the imperial court at Constantinople, with which the Franks did, indeed, have some diplomatic contact in his time. This apart, the only piece of contemporary information he shared with Evagrius was knowledge of the accession of Gregory I to the papacy in 590. For the rest, Gregory's world was confined to Gaul and its fringes; even Britain was a distant land of hearsay. Evagrius, though his horizons were wide enough to take in the Eastern Mediterranean, knew no more about Western Europe than Gregory knew about the East. While he had his copy of Procopius open before him he was made aware by it of the West. How little it impinged on his experience or excited his interest is clear from the narrative of his later books, concerned with his own days; he was aware that Pope Gregory succeeded Pelagius II in 590, and that is about all. In Rome in the 590s it was difficult to find anybody to translate letters from the Greek; even Pope Gregory, who had spent some years as the previous pope's representative in Constantinople, never learnt the language. The idealized image of an ecumenical empire could co-exist with a remarkable degree of parochialism.

In the culture of Western Europe the retirement of Cassiodorus (see above, pp. 159–60) was a landmark. Cassiodorus could no longer take for granted the widely diffused education, literacy, and a shared culture among the educated as a ubiquitous fact in the way that Augustine could take these for granted; now they had to be deliberately fostered. Some fine buildings, some magnificent mosaic decoration and ivory work appeared within the orbit of the Byzantine presence in Italy, mainly in Ravenna, and the popes built and adorned a few churches in Rome. Italy remained, for a while, something of a clearing house for trade and culture. But henceforward, in every field of thought and letters, in art and architecture, in theology and philosophy, until the revivals in one or other of the barbarian kingdoms, the West was to mark time. Cassiodorus tells us sadly of the collapse of his plans for the founding of a Christian university in Rome in 535: 'With the raging of war [the Gothic wars] and confusion in Italy my desires could in no way be realized. . . .'⁶ Cassiodorus removed his books to his monastic community in southern Italy, whence they were dispersed. Only a few of them have left a trace in subsequent history. The library of Christian classics established by Pope Agapetus, Cassiodorus' collaborator in his plans, survived; somehow it got incorporated in the complex of buildings around the family home of Gregory the Great, in the course of extensions made to it in order to accommodate his monastic community. An inscription recorded that in it Gregory composed his *Dialogues*. Its contents were in all probability moved to the papal archives, whether because the space was needed for monastic purposes, or because the monks had little use for them, we shall never know. It does not seem likely that they were intensively used in their new quarters; perhaps the books were buried by the archivists, perhaps there were not enough to make a working collection. At any rate, when it came to looking up fourth-century heresies, the necessary books could not be found in Rome and Gregory had to send to Ravenna.

Pope Gregory the Great was one of the last outstanding Westerners whose imagination could still embrace both the Greek world and the fragmented West of barbarian kingdoms; whose mind and culture belonged to the ancient world as well as to medieval Europe. Two strands were interwoven in the way he conceived the place of the Church in Christian society. One linked him with the dominant tradition of the previous 250 years: the tradition of a Roman, imperial Christianity. The other, the idea of a Christianity not linked to Roman values and not embodied exclusively in Roman society, though anticipated in theory, had made less headway before Gregory. So far as the sphere of the Empire was concerned, Gregory slipped easily into thinking of the Church's place in its life in the way that this had become defined over nearly three centuries. The threads, finally, had been gathered, in the generation before Gregory, by Emperor Justinian. His legislation rounded off the development of an 'imperial Church'. The Church, now a public power of the first importance, was also exposed to the active interest of the emperor and the government. The emperor as the head of a Christian empire was responsible for the purity of its faith and its life. Justinian's legislation not only enunciated this view, but embodied it by making detailed provision for countless ecclesiastical matters, from faith in the Holy Trinity to arrangements for the admission of postulants to monastic communities. So long as the emperor's orthodoxy was not in doubt, this image of the Church was generally accepted. Gregory's thought was dominated by it; within the orbit where the emperor's writ still ran, Gregory never questioned the framework of the imperial state-Church. Even occasional conflict with the emperor over some question of religion was kept, when it arose, within this framework. When the emperor enacted a new law restricting entry into the monastic profession, Gregory objected, and sent a passionate protest to the emperor; but he also circulated its provisions among Western bishops. To the emperor he wrote: 'Being subject to your orders I have had this law sent to various parts of the world; but because the law is by no means agreeable to Almighty God, I have made this known to your serene majesty by means of this representation. I have thus done my duty on both sides: I have obeyed the emperor and not kept silence as to my conscience before God.'[7] His protests against particular actions of the emperor are *ad hoc*, kept carefully on a personal level. Nothing could be more characteristic of Gregory's refusal to question the institutional framework of the Empire and the role it assigned to emperors and bishops in the life of the Church.

The Empire was still the 'Christian Commonwealth' and the unquestioned setting for Gregory's thought and actions, but it no longer filled his world. The collapse of imperial administration in the West, the disintegration of Roman social order and the chronic insecurity of Italian life under the pressure of the conquering Lombards turned Gregory's mind to the imminent end of the world. He was Roman enough to be apt to see the collapse of the Empire in such dramatic, apocalyptic terms. But the thought was not a cry of despair; on the contrary, it liberated Gregory's imagination from confinement within the horizon of empire. In Rome, and Italy, he had as a matter of course assumed all the diverse functions which were falling on the shoulders of the clergy in a society in which civil administration was running down. But unlike Roman bishops in Gaul a hundred years before, he no longer saw his task in terms of the preservation of the way of life of a Roman élite in a sea of barbarism. He had come to terms with the existence of barbarian kingdoms in Gaul, Spain and Britain; he was more clear-sighted than the government in realizing that the barbarians who were now established in Italy were also there to stay. His aim was not to drive them out, as the government still dreamed they could be; nor to mark out an enclave in which Roman life could be perpetuated in its traditional forms. His aim was to come to terms with the barbarians at the doorstep, to convert them to Christianity and to ease their way to membership of a peaceful Christian society.

Christian and Roman were no longer synonymous for him. Augustine had tried to drive a wedge into the imperial theology which identified the two concepts; but where

Augustine's theology failed, the tide of events and Gregory's pastoral imagination succeeded. Christendom was not to remain confined within the horizons of the Roman world. The Gospel had to be preached to pagan Anglo-Saxons. The churches of the Franks in Gaul or of the Goths in Spain were only too clearly no longer part of the state-Church of the Empire, but churches whose life was closely identified with their own kingdoms. What mattered to Gregory was that the quality of Christian life should be maintained in them. It would be wrong to credit Gregory with the notion of a supra-national European Christendom, a Latin Christian commonwealth centred on papal Rome; that notion is at once too abstract and too political to fit into his cast of mind. What he saw was a number of barbarian peoples who all needed to be saved by the Gospel message. That a society wholly dominated by the Church and a culture moulded almost entirely by churchmen eventually emerged in Western Europe may have been a remote consequence of his initiatives, especially in converting the English to Christianity. But his own imagination was not confined within the imperial mould. And it had not yet created the alternative mould which would come to confine the mental horizons of generations of Western Christians, no less disastrously, in the medieval centuries with an image of a Western, Rome-centred, Latin Christendom, its secular life directed by the Church, its institutions moulded by Christianity, its culture transmitted to it by the Church.

In almost every way we can see the parting ways mirrored in the career of Gregory the Great: the relentless, steady removal of Western Europe from the orbit of the Empire and, along with it, the isolation of the Latin Church and of Western culture. His own writings also show, perhaps more than any other body of literature, the Janus faces of a man who belonged to the world of medieval Europe as much as to antiquity. His letters abound in the courtesies and the artificialities which the imperial civil service had inculcated for generations – indeed, that had been the origin of the procedures of the papal writing office. His sermons, and even more his handbook of conduct for the clergy, the *Rule of Pastoral Care*, display a mind saturated with the thought of the Fathers, especially of Augustine. But Gregory inhabits a changed world, and the change is plain in the very texture of his writing. Once he compared the 'deep and clear torrents of the blessed fathers Ambrose and Augustine' with his own 'mean little trickle'; but the difference lay as much in the new public. The men of letters, lay and cleric, who read Ambrose's sermons on the Pentateuch or Augustine's *City of God* were gone. Gregory's 'mean little trickle' was better suited to quenching more modest thirsts. His *Dialogues*, especially, catered for unsophisticated minds in search of evidences of the holy in a chaotic world. Along with what they were seeking, they also got something of the old Roman sense of order, dignity and humanity.

Behold, we are watching the ruin of all this world, predicted in the Holy Scriptures: towns laid waste, fortified villages demolished, churches destroyed, our lands bereft of cultivators.[8]

The Lombard conquerors in the neighbourhood of Rome in 593 seemed to Gregory to herald the coming end. It was not to be the end of the world; but a world was passing away. Christianity had been born into a world held in the bonds of the 'Augustan peace'. To the rich variety of cultures embraced within that political structure it had adapted itself in a variety of ways, and to them it made its own, equally varied, contributions. It had brought a new element of tension as well as a new unifying force to that world. Now the unity was breaking and some of the tensions snapped. Within little more than a century of Gregory's death the English Church, gratefully conscious of its debt to 'our own apostle, St Gregory',[9] was to become the leading spiritual power in Western Christendom. But by then Christendom had been deprived of the flourishing Christian provinces of Africa, Egypt and the Middle East. In the last months of Gregory's pontificate an unprepossessing soldier, Phocas, obtained the throne of Constantinople after exterminating the imperial family. His reign was seen by his Greek subjects as a nightmare of brutality and degradation. We shall never know what prejudices – or what ignorance – enabled Gregory to write warmly to this 'savage and murderous monster of tyranny'[10] welcoming his accession to the throne. Not long after Gregory's death a column was erected in honour of Phocas in the Roman Forum. It stands near the spot which had seen the devoted labours of restoration by the last pagan aristocrats. There it marks the final eclipse of the traditions they had striven to keep alive; it marks also the end of a single, universal, Roman *cikoumene*.

Gregory saw the fate of Rome reflected in the prophecy of Ezechiel: '"Therefore thus saith the Lord God: Woe to the bloody city, of which I will make a bonfire. Heap together the bones and I will burn them in a great fire and the flesh shall be consumed . . ." (Ez. 24:9–10). Where now is the Senate? where the people? . . . the men are gone, the walls, too, are falling. Where are they who once rejoiced in her glory? . . . and what we say of Rome's fate, we know is also befalling other cities. . . .'[11] Behind the ruin Gregory saw the fragmentation and the moral collapse of his world: the Roman world. With him Christianity enters on a new era of its existence.

Notes to the text

PREFACE
1 Orosius, *Historiarum adversus paganos*, V.2.

1 A SECT AMONG SECTS
1 Tacitus, *Annals*, XV.44.
2 Aelius Aristides, *Roman oration*, 28, 94, 96, 97 quoted from the translation by J. H. Oliver, *The Ruling Power* (Trans. Amer. Philos. Soc. 43 (1953) 871–1003, at pp. 898, 905–6).
3 *Epistula ad Diognetum* 1.
4 As in Aristides, *Apologia* 2.1, according to the reading of some of the MSS.

2 THE THIRD RACE
1 xxxix.13.14.
2 Tertullian, *Scorpiace* 10.
3 *Annals* XV.44.
above, pp.
4 Origen, *Contra Celsum*, viii.2.
5 Minucius Felix, *Octavius* 8.
6 Origen, *Contra Celsum* I.1.
7 *Conversion*, pp. 16, 163.
8 Pliny, *Epistulae* x.96.
9 *Epistula ad Diognetum* 5.
10 *Enneades* I.4.7.
11 *ibid.* 1.6.8, quoting *Iliad* ii.140 – out of context.
12 *Sent. Sext.* 230b, 239.
13 Socrates, *Historia ecclesiastica* i.11.
14 e.g. *Sent. Sext.* 70.
15 *Dialogus*, 2.3–6.
16 *ibid.* 8.1–2.
17 *De vera religione* 5.8.
18 *Epistula* 234.2.

19 Origen, *Contra Celsum* i.2.
20 *Oratio ad Graecos* 25.
21 *ibid.* 1.
22 Eusebius, *Historia ecclesiastica* vi.19.7.
23 *Stromata* vi.89.
24 *Oratio panegyrica* xiii, *PG* 10.1096A.
25 *ibid.* vi, 1069C.

3 THE CRISIS OF IDENTITY
1 *Apologeticum* 46.
2 *De praescriptione hereticorum* 7.
3 *ibid.* 8.
4 *ibid.* 9.
5 *De carne Christi* 5.
6 Origen, *Contra Celsum* v.41, trans. H. Chadwick, p. 297.
7 *Apologeticum* 6.
8 *Adversus Valentinianos* 1.
9 *Contra haereses* iv.5.1.
10 *ibid.* i.10.3.
11 Eusebius, *Historia ecclesiastica* iii.32.7–8.
12 *Contra Celsum* iii.11–16.
13 *Didache* 11.7.

4 TOWARDS RESPECTABILITY
1 *Historia ecclesiastica* viii.1, trans. G. A. Williamson, Penguin ed. pp. 327–8.
2 Lactantius, *De mortibus persecutorum* 12 and Cyprian, *Epistola* 80.2.
3 *Contra Celsum* iii.15.
4 R. MacMullen, *Enemies of the Roman order* (1967), p. 229.

5 P. Brown, 'Christianity and local culture in late Roman Africa', *JRS* 58 (1968) pp. 85–95 at 91–2.
6 *Octavius* 5.4.
7 Lactantius, *De mortibus persecutorum* 34.
8 *Historia ecclesiastica* ix.7. 16.

5 THE CONSTANTINIAN REVOLUTION
1 *Historia ecclesiastica* x.1.8.
2 Eusebius, *De vita Constantini* ii.56, 60.
3 Olympiodorus, frag. 23, 34.
4 Symmachus, *Epistulae* i. 52.
5 Eusebius, *De vita Constantini* ii.28.
6 *ibid.* ii.55.
7 For an outstandingly instructive study of this two-way process see the paper by S. MacCormack, 'Change and continuity in late antiquity: the ceremony of *adventus*', *Historia* 21 (1972).
8 Though the emperor took an interest in their training and status: see *Cod. Theod.* xiii.4.1, 2.

6 PROTEST AND ESTABLISHMENT
1 *Acta Saturn.* 2.
2 *Apologeticum* 18.
3 *De pudicitia* 21.
4 *Historia ecclesiastica* vi. 43.1.

Notes to the text

5 *Epistulae* 66.8.3.
6 *ibid.* 55.8.5.
7 *ibid.* 69.2.1.
8 *ibid.* 71.2.4.
9 Psalm 96.1–2, quoted in *Historia ecclesiastica* x.1.3 (added in the last recension).
10 *De civitate Dei* v.24.

7 THE CHRISTIAN TIMES AND THE ROMAN PAST
1 *De vita Constantini* iv.54.
2 E. M. Wightman, *Roman Trier and the Treveri* (1970), pp. 229, 238.
3 Ammianus Marcellinus, xxi.10.8.
4 Zosimus, iv.59.
5 *Confessiones* i.13.22.
6 *Historia ecclesiastica* iii.16.

8 THE TRIUMPH OF CHRISTIANITY AND BARBARISM

1 Optatus, *De schismate Donatistarum adversus Parmenianum* iii.3.
2 *Contra Symmachum* i.523.
3 *ibid.* ii.585–636.
4 *Historiarum adversus paganos* vii.41.
5 *Carmina* xii.
6 *Epistulae* viii.2.1.
7 *ibid.* vi.17.1.
8 Cf. *Epistulae* 369.9, ed. Förster, vol. 10, p. 355, 1.20f.
9 *Epistulae* iv.17.2.
10 *Contra Symmachum* ii. 816–7.
11 xxxi.8.9; 15.2.
12 *Epistulae* i.5.2.
13 *ibid.* iv.1.4.
14 *ibid.* i.2.6.
15 *ibid.* vii.6.6.
16 *Vita Severini* 5.2.

9 THE PARTING WAYS
1 *Ambigua* 221b–222a.

2 G. Mathew, *Byzantine aesthetics* (1963), p. 54.
3 *Vita Melaniae junioris*, 53.
4 See Alan and Averil Cameron, 'Christianity and tradition in the historiography of the late Empire', *Class. Quart.* N.S. 14 (1964), pp. 316–28.
5 'The thought-world of East Rome', in *Byzantine studies and other essays* (1955), p. 142.
6 *Institutiones divinarum et saecularium litterarum, Praef.*
7 *Epistulae* iii.61.
8 *ibid.* iii.29; see also *Homilies on Ezechiel* i.9.9 and ii.6.22.
9 Bede, *Historia ecclesiastica* ii.1.
10 George of Pisidia, *Avar war* 49; see also *Heraclius* ii.5–11.
11 *Homilies on Ezechiel* ii.6.22, 24.

Bibliographical note

I have not been able to take account in this note of any material (other than that known to be forthcoming) published since the final completion of my typescript at Easter, 1972.

GENERAL
On early Christianity and the world around it: *The Crucible of Christianity*, ed. A. Toynbee (1969) contains some excellent introductory essays, richly illustrated. Also useful: F. van der Meer and C. Mohrmann, *Atlas of the Early Christian World* (1958). The best short history of the early Church is H. Chadwick, *The Early Church* (Pelican History of the Church, vol. 1, 1967). For more detail, see R. M. Grant, *Augustus to Constantine* (1971). The later period is not so well catered for; the older works by Duchesne, Lietzmann or in the Fliche and Martin *Histoire de l'Église* are still the best guides.

For the Roman world, F. Millar and others, *The Roman empire and its neighbours* (1967) is excellent for the third century. J. Vogt, *The Decline of Rome* (1967) and A. H. M. Jones, *The Decline of the Ancient World* (1966), based on his exhaustive work, *The Later Roman*

Empire (1964) are the best accounts. Sir Samuel Dill's *Roman society in the last century of the Western Empire* (1910²) is a perceptive and very readable work. Peter Brown, *The World of Late Antiquity* (1971) is a brilliant essay in interpretation.

There are many translations of works of the fathers and other contemporary sources, and commentaries on them and monographs on their authors. These can be found in more specialized bibliographies. Two good collections of documents, both edited by J. Stevenson: *A New Eusebius* (1957) and *Creeds, Councils and Controversies* (1966) cover the pre- and post-Nicene periods respectively.

ASPECTS OF CHRISTIANITY
J. Pelikan, *The Christian tradition: a history of the development of doctrine*, 1: The emergence of the Catholic tradition, 100–600 (1971), is outstanding. J. N. D. Kelly, *Early Christian doctrines* (1958) and *Early Christian creeds* (1950); G. L. Prestige, *Fathers and heretics* (1940); S. L. Greenslade, *Schism in the early Church* (1964²); P. R. Ackroyd and C. F. Evans, eds., *The Cambridge history of the Bible*, vol. 1 (1970); A. H. Armstrong, ed., *Cam-

bridge history of later Greek and early medieval philosophy* (1971²); J. Jungmann, *The early liturgy* (1959) are among the best introductions to their various fields. W. H. C. Frend, *Martyrdom and Persecution in the Early Church* (1965) is a wide-ranging and fascinating study of the first three centuries. A. Atiyah, *A history of Eastern Christianity* (1968) is a good survey of a field largely neglected in the present book. The series begun under the editorship of the late G. Le Bras, *Histoire du droit et des institutions de l'Église* (1955–) is much more than a history of canon law and institutions.

On Christianity and classical culture, the book of that title by C. N. Cochrane (1940) is stimulating. (See also under chapter 2.) On early Christian art and architecture: R. Krautheimer, *Early Christian and Byzantine architecture* (1965) is magisterial; of art, good accounts with excellent illustrations can be found in W. F. Volbach, *Early Christian Art* (1961) and A. Grabar, *The Beginnings of Christian Art* (1967). As the most stimulating studies of the social setting and function of art I would single out the following three books: H. P. L'Orange, *Art forms and civic* life in the late Roman Empire (1965); G. Mathew, *Byzantine aesthetics* (1963); and F. van der Meer, *Early Christian art* (1967).

F. Dvornik, *Early Christian and Byzantine political philosophy*, vol. 2 (1966) is a full history of a central theme.

1 A SECT AMONG SECTS

To fill the gap left at the beginning of this book, and to avoid the need to refer to a wide range of studies on New Testament times which I am ill-equipped to assess, I am content to refer only to C. H. Dodd, *The founder of Christianity* (1971), the distilled quintessence of a great scholar's work. For further orientation in the field, see M. Simon and A. Benoit, *Le Judaisme et le christianisme antique* (Nouvelle Clio 10, 1968). On the relations between Judaism and Christianity, M. Simon, *Verus Israel* (1948); on fourth-century anti-semitism, J. Parkes, 'Jews and Christians in the Constantinian Empire', *Studies in Church History* 1 (1964).

2 THE THIRD RACE

On Christian language, see C. Mohrmann's essays gathered in *Études sur le Latin des chrétiens* (1961–). On Christian and pagan religious attitudes the two outstanding works are A. D. Nock, *Conversion* (1933) and E. R. Dodds, *Pagan and Christian in an age of anxiety* (1965), on both of which I have leaned heavily in this chapter. On Christianity

and pagan thought, see H. Chadwick, *Early Christian thought and the classical tradition* (1966) and W. Jaeger, *Early Christianity and Greek paideia* (1962). A brief introduction to pagan religions in the Roman world: J. Ferguson, *The religions of the Roman Empire* (1970). The old work by C. Bigg, *The Christian Platonists of Alexandria* (1913) is still the best introduction to them in English, as is A. H. Armstrong, *The architecture of the intelligible universe in the philosophy of Plotinus* (1940) to the thought of pagan neo-Platonism. See also *Cambridge history of later Greek and early medieval philosophy* (see above, under 'General').

3 THE CRISIS OF IDENTITY

My interpretation of Gnosticism and the orthodox reaction to it is elaborated in my article 'Pleroma and fulfilment . . .', *Vigiliae christianae* 8 (1954). On heresy and orthodoxy, the classic of W. Bauer, *Orthodoxy and heresy in earliest Christianity* (1971) can now be read in an English translation. Important discussion of the question in H. E. W. Turner, *The pattern of Christian truth* (1954). On the idea of tradition, R. P. C. Hanson, *Tradition in the early Church* (1963) and Y. M. J. Congar, *La tradition et les traditions* (1960: this ranges widely). On apostolic succession, A. A. T. Ehrhardt, *The apostolic succession* (1953). On the NT canon, cf. ch. 10 in *Cambridge history of the Bible*, 1 (above), by R. M. Grant; on its significance the essay on

'The Tradition' by O. Cullmann in *The early Church* (1956). On ecclesiastical office, H. von Campenhausen, *Ecclesiastical authority and spiritual power* (1969); J. Colson, *Les fonctions ecclésiales aux deux premiers siècles* (1956).

4 TOWARDS RESPECTABILITY

See general bibliography, and chapter 3.

5 THE CONSTANTINIAN REVOLUTION

On Constantine the best short expositions in English are A. H. M. Jones, *Constantine and the conversion of Europe* (1952) and R. MacMullen, *Constantine* (1970). On his role as a Christian ruler, N. H. Baynes, 'Constantine the Great and the Christian Church', in *Proc. Brit. Acad.* 15 (1929). A. Momigliano, ed., *The conflict of paganism and Christianity in the fourth century* (1963) contains some interesting and distinguished essays. A. H. M. Jones' chapter, 'The social background of the struggle between paganism and Christianity' is fundamental. S. L. Greenslade, *Church and state from Constantine to Theodosius* (1954) is a good short account.

6 PROTEST AND ESTABLISHMENT

W. H. C. Frend, *The Donatist Church* (1952) is a classic study; some of the necessary reservations on it are voiced by P. R. L. Brown, 'Religious dissent in the later

Roman Empire: the case of North Africa', in *History* 46 (1961). On the whole question, cf. my survey 'Christianity and dissent in Roman North Africa: new perspectives in recent work' in *Studies in Church history* 9 (1972). The finest work on Augustine is P. Brown, *Augustine of Hippo: a biography* (1967). I have defended my interpretation in *Saeculum: history and society in the theology of Saint Augustine* (1970).

7 THE CHRISTIAN TIMES AND THE ROMAN PAST
On Theodosius and the establishment of Christianity, a good short book under that title by N. Q. King (1961). On the pagan resistance and the conflict with Christianity, the older works by G. Boissier, *La fin du paganisme antique* (1894²); J. Geffcken, *Der Ausgang des griechisch-römischen Heidentums* (1920) and P. De Labriolle, *La réaction paienne* (1948). Cf. also Dill, *Roman society* (General, above), and Momigliano, ed., *The conflict . . .* (above, ch. 5), especially the essay by H. Bloch, 'The pagan revival in the West at the end of the fourth century'. H. I. Marrou, *Saint Augustin et la fin de la culture antique* (1938) is a classic on its theme. On the conversion of the aristocracy and the study of letters, P. Brown, 'Aspects of the christianization of the Roman aristocracy', *JRS* 51 (1961) and A. Cameron, 'The date and identity of Macrobius', *JRS*

56 (1966) are pioneering studies. I have discussed the subject in 'Paganism, Christianity and the Latin classics' in *Fourth century Latin*, ed. J. W. Binns (1974). On editing and copying the classics: the standard account, now in need of revision, is still that by O. Jahn, 'Über die Subskriptionen in den Handschriften römischer Classiker', *Ber. über d. Verh. d. k. sächs. Ges. d. Wiss.*, *Phil-Hist. Cl.* 3 (1851). On the 'Sixtine renaissance': R. Krautheimer, 'The architecture of Sixtus III: a fifth century renaissance?' in *De artibus opuscule XL*, ed. M. Meiss (1961), now repr. in his *Studies in early Christian, medieval and Renaissance art* (1969).

8 THE TRIUMPH OF CHRISTIANITY AND BARBARISM
On Sidonius: C. E. Stevens, *Sidonius Apollinaris and his age* (1933); on the exclusiveness of Roman society, P. Brown, 'The Later Roman Empire', *Econ. Hist. rev.*, Essays in Bibliography and Criticism, 66; 2nd ser. 20 (1967) and J. M. Wallace Hadrill, 'Gothia and Romania', in *The Longhaired kings* (1962). On Severinus and his biographer, cf. L. Bieler's introduction to his translation of Eugippius' *Life of Severinus* (1965). On Cassiodorus, A. Momigliano, 'Cassiodorus and the Italian culture of his time', *Proc. Brit. Acad.* 41 (1955), repr. in his *Studies in history and historiography* (1969) is fun-

damental. M. Wes, *Das Ende des Kaisertums im West des römischen Reiches* (1967) is a suggestive interpretation of the tradition of senatorial ideas down to the Ostrogothic period.

9 THE PARTING WAYS
Byzantine history lies outside the scope of this book. The new edition of vol. 4 of the *Cambridge medieval history*, by J. M. Hussey and D. M. Nicol will provide the student with detail and bibliographies. I should like however to refer to the work of N. H. Baynes, greatest of Byzantinists, mentioned more than once in the text, and especially to his two brilliant essays, 'The Hellenistic civilization of East Rome', and 'The thought-world of East Rome', both repr. in his *Byzantine studies and other essays* (1955). On the theology of cosmic redemption and its absence in the West, see A. H. Armstrong, *St Augustine and the Augustinian tradition* (1967), repr. in *Augustine: a collection of critical essays*, ed. R. A. Markus (1972). The biography of Daniel the Stylite can be read in an English translation in *Three Byzantine Saints*, ed. E. Dawes and N. H. Baynes (1948). On the library of Agapetus, see H. I. Marrou, 'Autour de la bibliothèque du pape Agapit', *Mél. d'arch. et d'hist.* 48 (1937). The best interpretation of Gregory the Great is to be found in E. Caspar, *Geschichte des Papsttums*, vol. 2 (1933).

Index

Works mentioned only in the Bibliographical Note are not indexed.

Index